THE FUTURE OF WORK

Insights You Need from Harvard Business Review

Business is changing. Will you adapt or be left behind?

Get up to speed and deepen your understanding of the topics that are shaping your company's future with the **Insights You Need from Harvard Business Review** series. Featuring HBR's smartest thinking on fast-moving issues—blockchain, cybersecurity, AI, and more—each book in this series provides the foundation introduction and practical case studies your organization needs to compete today and collects the best research, interviews, and analysis to get it ready for tomorrow.

You can't afford to ignore how these issues will transform the landscape of business and society. The Insights You Need series will help you grasp these critical ideas—and prepare you and your company for the future.

Books in the series include:

Agile

Artificial Intelligence

Blockchain

Climate Change

Coronavirus: Leadership and Recovery

Customer Data and Privacy

Cybersecurity

The Future of Work

Global Recession

Monopolies and Tech Giants

Racial Justice

Strategic Analytics

The Year in Tech, 2021

The Year in Tech 2022

THE FUTURE OF WORK

Harvard Business Review Press
Boston, Massachusetts

Printed in the United States of America

10 9 8 7 6 5 4 3 2 1

Library of Congress Cataloging-in-Publication Data

Names: Harvard Business Review Press, issuing body.
Title: The future of work.
Other titles: Future of work (Harvard Business Review Press) | Insights you need from Harvard Business Review.
Description: Boston, Massachusetts : Harvard Business Review Press, [2021] | Series: Insights you need from Harvard Business Review | Includes index.
Identifiers: LCCN 2021021329 (print) | LCCN 2021021330 (ebook) | ISBN 9781647822286 (paperback) | ISBN 9781647822293 (ebook)
Subjects: LCSH: Quality of work life. | Corporate culture. | Diversity in the workplace. | Work environment—Moral and ethical aspects.
Classification: LCC HD6955 .F854 2021 (print) | LCC HD6955 (ebook) | DDC 658.3/12—dc23
LC record available at https://lccn.loc.gov/2021021329
LC ebook record available at https://lccn.loc.gov/2021021330

ISBN: 978-1-64782-228-6
eISBN: 879-1-64782-229-3

The paper used in this publication meets the requirements of the American National Standard for Permanence of Paper for Publications and Documents in Libraries and Archives Z39.48-1992.

Contents

Section 2
The New Workforce

Section 3
Redefining the Inclusive Organization

Section 4
The Purpose-Driven Organization

Introduction

THE NEW WORLD OF WORK

by Brian Kropp

In just a handful of months, the relationship between employers and employees has fundamentally transformed due to several factors. The impact of the social justice movement, the Covid-19 pandemic, and digital evolution have dramatically accelerated the pace of change. Leaders who think that what has happened across the last year has been a blip, and that we will return to "normal," are wrong. Much like heating water, this transformation is the result of factors that have been at play—slowly heating up—for years, and then in 2020 hit a full boil. The changes we have experienced, and will continue to experience, represent a fundamental shift to a new, different relationship between employees and employers. There is no going back.

The new deal between employees and employers will be redefined along a series of three dimensions: creating a shared purpose, radical flexibility, and deeper connections. The result will be organizations driving social change and improving diversity, equity, and inclusion (DE&I) efforts; employees exerting more control over where, when, and how much they work; and employers becoming more involved in supporting the life experience—not just the employment experience—of their employees.

A Shared DE&I Purpose

To create a more diverse, equitable, and inclusive organization, leaders must go beyond corporate messages to real behavior change. In order to drive DE&I in their organization, executives must model the right behaviors. But this is only step one: Executives must do more; they must use their budget, systems, and processes to drive DE&I throughout the organization.

Improving DE&I efforts within the four (virtual) walls of your organization is laudable, but your workforce expects more; three-quarters of employees expect their employer to take a stance on current societal and cultural issues, even if those issues have nothing to do with their business. CEOs commonly get involved by issuing a corporate statement in response to these issues. However, research has found that only issuing a corporate statement degrades employee engagement versus the status quo of doing nothing at all.[1] Instead, when organizations put actions behind their words—by reallocating resources, changing suppliers, giving employees time off to volunteer, and explaining these moves—the number of highly engaged employees increases. This is true even for employees who disagree with the organization's stance on the issue; while they might disagree, they at least know why the decision was made.

Radical Flexibility

Progressive organizations have embraced the idea of radical flexibility—giving employees control over where, when, and how much they work—to meet the desires of employees and realize the potential financial benefits of a hybrid workforce. Research shows that when employees are able to choose where, when, and how much they work, the number of high performers in a company can increase by as much as 19%.[2] Now the question is: How do we redesign work to achieve this? While experiments are playing out across companies, one of the major lessons is that leaders must shift to a much greater emphasis on the output employees achieve rather than the systems and processes they use to achieve it.

The pandemic has revealed that, for most employees, we can break the relationship between work and place. Yet, thoughtful executives realize that there is still a critical need for real estate. They are exploring how the "job" of their real estate should shift to support collaboration, reinforce culture, and create moments that engage their community and customers in different ways.

Deeper Connections

The Covid-19 pandemic has changed the depth of the relationship between employees and employers. Managers have learned more about the personal lives of their employees than they ever thought they would. Zoom calls revealed family members, pets, and kids. Conversations about physical well-being and mental health became the norm. The result is that employers are moving from trying to improve the employee experience of their staff to improving the life experience of the human beings who happen to work for them.

Companies are not just supporting their employees' lives through additional benefits like mental health and sleep support. They are pushing beyond that to have a deeper impact. For example, Novartis opened up its internal learning and development platform to employees' family members to help them learn new and necessary skills. These deeper connections pay off. Based on research, when organizations take this holistic approach, they can see a 23% increase in the number of employees reporting better mental health, a 17% increase in the number of employees reporting better physical health, and a 21% increase in the number of high performers.

What This Book Will Do

The nine articles in this book will help you manage the new landscape of work and examine how your organization can evolve to deliver improving outcomes for both employees and employers.

Section 1, "The Authentic, Anywhere Office," addresses several of the key issues of the new radically flexible workforce. This section moves beyond some of the initial concerns we had about a more flexible way of working and tackles concerns that range from supporting the mental health of our employees to ensuring we are delivering on our values. Section 2, "The New Workforce," challenges our very definition of who our employees are. As AI automates more roles and companies incorporate contract employees to an even greater degree, this raises a new set of frameworks and opportunities to create a different-in-kind workforce. Section 3, "Redefining the Inclusive Organization," paints the picture of how we need to evolve our DE&I strategies to not only be about communication but to also invest our budget dollars in real substantive change. Section 4, "The Purpose-Driven Organization," asks the question of how organizations should become more involved and build deeper connections with their employees and their communities to drive real, sustained change.

Today's new employment deal, centered on shared purpose, radical flexibility, and deeper connections, will define the future relationship between employees and employers. Organizations that get this right will have a more engaged and productive workforce, which will translate to a significant competitive advantage. Employees will be better off; employers will be better off. The articles in this collection will help you get started.

NOTES

1. Brian Kropp, "Gartner Opening Keynote: The New Employment Deal," filmed October 13, 2020, at the virtual Gartner ReimagineHR conference, via LinkedInLive, 27:35.

2. Ibid.

Section 1

THE AUTHENTIC, ANYWHERE OFFICE

OUR WORK-FROM-ANYWHERE FUTURE

by Prithwiraj (Raj) Choudhury

Before 2020 a movement was brewing within knowledge-work organizations. Personal technology and digital connectivity had advanced so far and so fast that people had begun to ask, "Do we really need to be together, in an office, to do our work?" We got our answer during the pandemic lockdowns. We learned that a great many of us don't in fact need to be colocated with colleagues on-site to do our jobs. Individuals, teams, and entire workforces can perform well while being entirely distributed—and they have. So now we face new questions: Are all-remote or majority-remote organizations the future of knowledge work? Is work from anywhere (WFA) here to stay?

Without question, the model offers notable benefits to companies and their employees. Organizations can reduce or eliminate real estate costs, hire and use talent globally while mitigating immigration issues, and, research indicates, perhaps enjoy productivity gains. Workers get geographic flexibility (that is, live where they prefer to), eliminate commutes, and report better work/life balance. However, concerns persist regarding how WFA affects communication, including brainstorming and problem-solving; knowledge sharing; socialization, camaraderie, and mentoring; performance evaluation and compensation; and data security and regulation.

To better understand how leaders can capture the upside of WFA while overcoming the challenges and avoiding negative outcomes, I've studied several companies that have embraced all- or majority-remote models. They include the United States Patent and Trademark Office, or USPTO (which has several thousand WFA workers); Tulsa Remote; Tata Consultancy Services, or TCS (a global IT services company that has announced a plan to be 75% remote by 2025); GitLab (the world's largest all-remote company, with 1,300 employees); Zapier (a workflow automation company with more than 300 employees, none of them colocated, around the United States and in 23 other countries); and MobSquad (a Canadian startup that employs WFA workers).

The Covid-19 crisis has opened senior leaders' minds to the idea of adopting WFA for all or part of their workforces. In addition to TCS, companies including Twitter, Facebook, Shopify, Siemens, and State Bank of India have announced that they will make remote work permanent even after widespread vaccine availability. Another organization I've studied is BRAC, one of the world's largest NGOs, which is headquartered in Bangladesh. Forced into remote work this year, it is deciding what work model to adopt for the long term.

If your organization is considering a WFA program, transition, or launch, this article can provide a guide.

A Short History of Remote Work

A large-scale transition from traditional, colocated work to remote work arguably began with the adoption of work-from-home (WFH) policies in the 1970s, as soaring gasoline prices caused by the 1973 OPEC oil embargo made commuting more expensive. Those policies allowed people to eschew physical offices in favor of their homes, coworking spaces, or other community locations, such as coffee shops and public libraries, for occasional days, on a regular part-time basis, or full-time, with the expectation that they would come into the office periodically. Workers were often also given control over their schedules, allowing them to make time for school pickups, errands, or midday exercise without being seen as shirking. They saved time by commuting less and tended to take fewer sick days.

Thanks to the advent of personal computers, the internet, email, broadband connectivity, laptops, cell phones, cloud computing, and videotelephony, the adoption of WFH increased in the 2000s. As the researchers Ravi S. Gajendran and David A. Harrison note in a 2007 article, this trend was accelerated by the need to comply with, for example, the Americans with Disabilities Act of 1990 and mandates of the U.S. Equal Employment Opportunity Commission.[1]

Research has shown performance benefits. A 2015 study by Nicholas Bloom and coauthors found that when employees opted in to WFH policies, their productivity increased by 13%.[2] When, nine months later, the same workers were given a choice between remaining at home and returning to the office, those who chose the former saw even further improvements: They were 22% more productive than they had been before the experiment. This suggests that people should probably determine for themselves the situation (home or office) that fits them best.

In recent years many companies have allowed more employees to work from home. It's true that several prominent corporations, including Yahoo and IBM, had reversed course before the pandemic, asking their employees to resume colocated work in a bid to spur more-effective collaboration. But other organizations—the ones I study—moved toward greater geographic flexibility, allowing some if not all employees, new and old, to work from anywhere, completely untethered to an office. The USPTO is a prime example. Its leaders launched a WFA program in 2012, building on an existing WFH program that mandated workers' physical presence at headquarters, in northern Virginia, at least one day a week. The WFA program, in contrast, requires employees to spend two years at HQ followed by a WFH phase, after which they may live anywhere in the continental United States, provided they're willing to pay out of pocket for periodic travel back to headquarters (totaling no more than

12 days a year). The patent examiners in the program dispersed all across the country, choosing to move closer to family, to better climates, or to places with a lower cost of living.

Most companies that offer WFH or WFA options keep some workers—at the USPTO it's trainees and administrators—at one or more offices. In other words, they are hybrid-remote operations. But the experiment with all-remote work forced by Covid-19 has caused some of these organizations to strategically move toward majority-remote, with fewer than 50% of employees colocated in physical offices. TCS, for example, which employs close to 418,000 people who were traditionally located either on campuses or at client sites around the world, has decided to adopt a 25/25 model: Employees will spend only 25% of their working hours in the office, and at no point will the company have more than 25% of workers colocated. TCS plans to complete this transition in five years.

Even before the crisis, a smaller group of companies had taken this trend a step further, eliminating offices altogether and dispersing everyone, from entry-level associates to the CEO. GitLab embraces this model at scale: Its remote workers span sales, engineering, marketing, personnel management, and executive roles in more than 60 countries.

Exploring the Benefits

I've spent the past five years studying the practices and productivity trends of WFA companies. The upsides—for individuals, companies, and society—are clear. Let me outline them.

For individuals

One striking finding is how greatly workers benefit from these arrangements. Many told me that they regard the freedom to live anywhere in the world as an important plus. For those in dual-career situations, it eases the pain of looking for two jobs in a single location. One patent examiner told me, "I'm a military spouse, which means I live in a world with frequent moves and personal upheavals that prevent many spouses from pursuing lasting careers of their choice. WFA has been the most meaningful telework program I have encountered. It allows me to follow my husband to any U.S. state at a moment's notice and pursue my own aspirations to contribute to my home and society."

Some cited a better quality of life. "WFA has allowed my children to see their grandparents on a regular basis and play with their cousins," I heard from another USPTO employee. "Being closer to family has improved my overall happiness." Others talked about proximity to medical care for children, accommodating their partners, and the ability to enjoy warmer weather, prettier views, and greater recreational opportunities. Millennials in particular seemed captivated by the idea that WFA would allow them to become "digital nomads," traveling the world while still employed. Before the pandemic-related restrictions, some companies, such as Remote Year, were aiming to facilitate that lifestyle, and some countries, such as Estonia and Barbados, have created a new class of employment visa for such workers. As one patent examiner said, "Participation in [WFA] is outstanding for work/life balance. I live in my favorite part of the country . . . I have more time to relax."

Cost of living was another frequent theme. Because the USPTO did not adjust salaries according to where employees chose to live, one patent examiner told me, "I was able to buy a large home in my new location for about a quarter of the cost in northern Virginia." Some localities, such as the state of Vermont and the city of Tulsa, Oklahoma (where Tulsa Remote is located), have made a concerted effort to lure remote workers, touting the local community and lower costs. In San Francisco the average rent on a two-bedroom apartment is $4,128; in Tulsa it's a mere $675.

WFA also helps knowledge workers deal with immigration issues and other restrictions on their ability to secure good jobs. William Kerr, Susie Ma, and I recently studied MobSquad, whose coworking spaces in Halifax, Calgary, and other cities enable talented knowledge workers to bypass the onerous U.S. visa and green card system and instead obtain fast-track work permits from Canada's Global Talent Stream. Thus they can continue serving companies and clients in the United States and other countries while living and paying taxes in Canada.

One engineer we interviewed had come to the United States after graduating from high school in his home country at the age of 12. At age 16 he enrolled at a U.S. university, where he acquired degrees in math, physics, and computer science in three years. By age 19 he was employed at a medical tech company through the optional practical training (OPT) program, but he failed to get an H-1B visa and faced deportation. MobSquad moved him to Calgary, and he kept working with the same employer.

In interviews with female employees at BRAC, I learned that women whose careers were previously limited by cultural taboos against traveling to remote places or delegating housework had been helped by WFA. As one explained, "Earlier I had to wake up early in the morning and cook three meals for my intergenerational family. Working remotely has allowed me to spread out the household work, get extra sleep, and be more productive."

For organizations

My research also uncovered ample organizational benefits from WFA programs. For example, they increase employee engagement—an important metric of success for any company. In 2013, a year after it instituted work from anywhere, the USPTO was ranked highest on the Best Places to Work in the Federal Government survey.

Workers are not only happier but also more productive. When Cirrus Foroughi, Barbara Larson, and I evaluated the USPTO's transition from WFH to WFA, the timing of which happened at random for workers who'd chosen that path, we found that WFA boosted individual productivity by 4.4%, as measured by the number of patents examined each month.[3] The switch also led examiners to exert greater effort. Of course, further research is needed to determine whether WFA generates similar benefits for workers performing different tasks in other team structures and organizations.

Some gains generated by WFA are more obvious. For example, fewer in-office employees means smaller space requirements and reduced real estate costs. The USPTO estimated that increases in remote work in 2015 saved it $38.2 million. WFA programs also hugely expand an organization's potential talent pool to include workers tied to a location far from that of the company. That's a primary reason for the adoption at TCS of what it calls *secure borderless workspaces*, or SBWs: It wants to ensure that every project is staffed by employees with the right skills, no matter where they are. Rajesh Gopinathan, the CEO, describes this model as "talent on the cloud," while another senior executive says it will potentially allow the company to tap niche labor markets, such as Eastern Europe, that have a large supply of skilled financial analysts and data scientists.

Finally, WFA can reduce attrition. Some USPTO workers explained that because they loved their preferred locales but also recognized the limited job opportunities there, they were motivated to work harder and stay longer with the Patent Office. Leaders at GitLab, too, pointed to employee retention as a positive outcome of the company's decision to be all-remote. The net benefit, they believe, including the productivity increases and property cost savings they've seen, equals $18,000 a year for each worker.

For society

WFA organizations have the potential to reverse the brain drain that often plagues emerging markets, small towns, and rural locations. In fact, Tulsa Remote was established to attract diverse, energetic, community-minded newcomers to a city still healing from historic race riots a century ago. With an offer of $10,000 to relocate to Tulsa, the company attracted more than 10,000 applications for just 250 slots from 2019 to 2020. Obum Ukabam was one of the workers chosen. When he's not busy with his day job as a marketing manager, he mentors and coaches a local high school debate team. Talented newcomers of varied ethnicities are arguably making the city more multicultural. Meanwhile, the transitions at the USPTO and TCS have brought many people back to their hometowns.

Remote work helps the environment as well. In 2018 Americans' commute time averaged 27.1 minutes each way, or about 4.5 hours a week. Eliminating that commute—particularly in places where most people commute by car—generates a significant reduction in emissions. The USPTO estimates that in 2015 its remote workers drove 84 million fewer miles than if they had been traveling to headquarters, reducing carbon emissions by more than 44,000 tons.

Addressing the Concerns

The office—with its meeting rooms and break areas and opportunities for both formal and informal interaction—has been a way of life for so long that it's hard to imagine getting rid of it. And legitimate hurdles exist to making all-remote work not only manageable but successful. However, the Covid-19 all-remote experiment has taught many knowledge-work organizations and their employees that with time and attention, those concerns can be addressed. And in the companies I've studied, several best practices are emerging.

Communication, brainstorming, and problem-solving

When workers are distributed, synchronous communication becomes more difficult. Tools such as Zoom, Skype, Microsoft Teams, and Google Hangouts can help for those working in the same or similar time zones but not for those spread farther apart. In research with Jasmina Chauvin and Tommy Pan Fang, I found that when changing to or from daylight saving time caused a one- to two-hour reduction in business-hour overlap (BHO) between offices of a very large global corporation, the volume of communication fell by 9.2%, primarily among production workers. When BHO was greater, R&D staffers conducted more unplanned synchronous calls. Group meetings are even harder to schedule. Nadia Vatalidis of GitLab's People Operations group says that having team members in Manila, Nairobi, Johannesburg, Raleigh, and Boulder made finding a time for their weekly group call nearly impossible.

WFA organizations must therefore get comfortable with asynchronous communication, whether through a Slack channel, a customized intracompany portal, or even a shared Google document in which geographically distributed team members write their questions and comments and trust that other team members in distant time zones will respond at the first opportunity. One benefit to this approach is that employees are more likely to share early-stage ideas, plans, and documents and to welcome early feedback; the pressure to present polished work is less than it would be in more formal, synchronous team meetings. GitLab calls this process *blameless problem-solving.* The company's leaders note that employees accustomed to a culture of emails, phone calls, and meetings may struggle to change old habits; they solve that problem with training during onboarding and beyond. At Zapier, in a program called Zap Pal, each new hire is matched with an experienced buddy who sets up at least one introductory Zoom call and continues to check in throughout the first month. For synchronous brainstorming the company uses video calls and online whiteboards such as Miro, Stormboard, IPEVO Annotator, Limnu, and MURAL but also urges employees to use asynchronous means of problem-solving through Slack channel threads.

Knowledge sharing

This is another challenge for all-remote or majority-remote organizations. Distributed colleagues can't tap one another on the shoulder to ask questions or get help. Research by Robin Cowan, Paul David, and Dominique Forayhas postulated that much workplace knowledge is not codified (even when it can be) and instead resides "in people's heads."[4] This is a problem for all organizations, but much more so for those that have embraced WFA. The companies I've studied solve it with transparent and easily accessible documentation. At GitLab all team members have access to a "working handbook," which some describe as "the central repository for how we run the company." It currently consists of 5,000 searchable pages. All employees are encouraged to add to it and taught how to create a new topic page, edit an existing one, embed video, and so forth. Ahead of meetings, organizers post agendas that link to the relevant sections to allow invitees to read background information and post questions. Afterward recordings of the sessions are posted on GitLab's YouTube channel, agendas are edited, and the handbook is updated to reflect any decisions made.

Employees may see the extra work of documentation as a "tax" and balk at the extremely high level of transparency necessary for a WFA organization to thrive. Thorsten Grohsjean and I have argued that senior managers must set an example on these fronts by codifying knowledge and freely sharing information while explaining that these are necessary trade-offs to allow for geographic flexibility.

A related idea is to create transcripts, publicly post slides, and record video seminars, presentations, and meetings to create a repository of such material that individuals can view asynchronously at their convenience. For its 2020 annual meeting, which was forced by the pandemic to go virtual, the Academy of Management curated 1,120 prerecorded sessions, arguably expanding the flow of knowledge to scholars—especially those in emerging markets—far more than would have been possible at the in-person event, which typically happens in North America.

Socialization, camaraderie, and mentoring

Another major worry, cited by managers and workers alike, is the potential for people to feel isolated socially and professionally, disconnected from colleagues and the company itself, particularly in organizations where some people are colocated and some are not. Research by Cecily D. Cooper and Nancy B. Kurland has shown that remote workers often feel cut off from the information flow they would typically get in a physical office.[5] Without in-person check-ins, managers may miss signs of growing burnout or team dysfunction. Even with videoconferencing that allows for reading body language and facial expressions, the concern is that virtual colleagues are less likely to become close friends because their face-to-face interactions are less frequent. As GitLab's technical evangelist Priyanka Sharma put it, "I was very nervous when I was first thinking of joining, because I was very social in the office. I worried that I would be so lonely at home and wouldn't have that community feel." Houda Elyazgi, a marketing executive on the Tulsa Remote team, expressed similar sentiments: "Remote work can be very isolating, especially for introverts. You almost have to create an intentional experience when you're socializing with others. And then you have to be 'on' all the time, even when you're trying to relax. That's taxing."

In my research I've seen a range of policies that seek to address these concerns and create opportunities for socialization and the spreading of company norms. Many WFA organizations rely on technology to help facilitate virtual watercoolers and "planned randomized interactions," whereby someone in the company schedules groups of employees to chat online. Some use AI and virtual reality tools to pair up remote colleagues for weekly chats. For example, Sike Insights is using data on individual communication styles and AI to create Slackbot buddies, while eXp Realty, an all-remote company I'm currently researching, uses a VR platform called VirBELA to create a place for distant team members to gather in avatar form.

Sid Sijbrandij, a cofounder and the CEO of GitLab, told me, "I know at Pixar they placed the restroom centrally so people would bump into each other—but why depend on randomness for that? Why not step it up a notch and actually organize the informal communication?" These "mixers" often include senior and C-suite executives. When I described them to my HBS colleague Christina Wallace, she gave them a nice name: *community collisions.* And companies have always needed to manufacture them: Research dating back to Thomas J. Allen's work at MIT in the 1970s shows that workers colocated on the same "campus" may not experience serendipitous interactions if they are separated by a wall, a ceiling, or a building.

When it comes to interaction between people at different hierarchical levels, my research has revealed two problems with straightforward solutions. Iavor Bojinov, Ashesh Rambachan, and I found that the senior leaders of a global firm were often too stretched to offer one-on-one mentoring to virtual workers. So we implemented a Q&A process whereby workers posed questions through a survey and leaders responded asynchronously. Senior managers at another global firm told me that they had difficulty being themselves on camera. Whereas young remote workers were "living their lives on Instagram," their older colleagues found virtual engagement harder. The company implemented coaching sessions to make those executives more comfortable on Microsoft Teams.

Another solution to the socialization problem is to host "temporary colocation events," inviting all workers to spend a few days with colleagues in person. Prior to Covid-19, Zapier hosted two of those a year, paying for employee flights, accommodation, and food; giving teams an activities budget; and sending people home with $50 to use on a thank-you gift for their loved ones. Carly

Moulton, the company's senior communications specialist, told me, "Personally, I have made a lot of friendships with the people I travel to and from the airport with. The event managers will put us into random groups based on what time you arrive and depart. I've always been with people I don't normally work with, so it's nice to have a dedicated time when you have to make conversation."

Finally, at the USPTO, I learned another way to create camaraderie. Several WFA examiners have voluntarily created "remote communities of practice" so that a handful of them can get together periodically. A group living in North Carolina, for example, decided to schedule meetings on a golf course to socialize, discuss work, and problem-solve together. Another manager created a "virtual meal" by ordering the same pizza for delivery to the homes of all remote direct reports during a weekly team call.

Performance evaluation and compensation

How can you rate and review employees you're never physically with, particularly on "soft" but important metrics such as interpersonal skills? All-remote companies evaluate remote workers according to the quality of their work output, the quality of virtual interactions, and feedback from clients and colleagues. Zapier, for example, uses Help Scout for customer support replies; a feature of this software is that customers can submit a "happiness score" by rating the response as "great," "OK," or "not good."

In the spring and summer of 2020, as groups suddenly transitioned to remote work, I was asked whether managers should use software to track worker productivity and prevent shirking. I am very much opposed to this Orwellian approach. The USPTO addressed claims of "examiner fraud" and "attendance abuse" in its WFA program following a review by the U.S. Commerce Department's Office of the Inspector General. Those claims involved either overreporting of hours worked or shifts in the time logs of completed work, such as backloading at the end of a calendar quarter—neither of which related to the metric on which performance was measured: the number of patents examined. Nevertheless, from then on, all USPTO teleworkers had to use organizational IT tools, such as logging in to a virtual private network (VPN), having a presence indicator turned on, and using the same messaging services. But when we compared data from before and after that intervention, we found that it had no effect on average output.

How to set compensation for workers who work from anywhere is an active and interesting debate. As mentioned, it's a benefit to be able to reside in a lower-cost-of-living locale while earning the income one would in a more expensive one. But that's conditional on the company's not adjusting wages according to where a worker lives, as was the case at the USPTO. Matt Mullenweg, the founder of Automattic (parent of WordPress), another all-remote company, told me that its policy is to pay the same wages for the same roles, regardless of location. But GitLab and other companies do have different pay for different geographies, taking into account the experience of the worker, the contract type, and the task being performed. Although research is needed on which approach is optimal, it's possible that companies that tie wages to location will lose high-quality WFA workers to rivals that don't. Another pertinent issue is whether to pay WFA workers in the currency of the country where the organization is incorporated or the local one, in part to ensure consistent wages across locations over time, given exchange-rate fluctuations.

Data security and regulation

Several managers told me that cybersecurity was a big area of focus for WFA programs and organizations. "What if the WFA worker takes photographs of client data screens and sends them to a competitor?" one asked. The CIOs of some companies with remote-work policies said another key concern was employees' use of personal, less-protected devices for work at home.

It's true that all-remote companies have to work harder to protect employee, corporate, and customer data. As TCS transitions to a majority-remote model, it has moved from "perimeter-based security" (whereby the IT team attempts to secure every device) to "transaction-based security" (whereby machine learning algorithms analyze any abnormal activities on any employee laptop). MobSquad has replicated its client security infrastructure for WFA workers, and employees work on clients' cloud, email, and hardware in its offices for security reasons. All-remote and majority-remote organizations I have studied are experimenting with a wide range of solutions to protect client data using predictive analytics, data visualization, and computer vision.

Transitioning to an all-remote or a majority-remote organization sometimes requires jumping regulatory hurdles as well. At the onset of the pandemic, when TCS was forced to become all-remote, it had to work with NASSCOM (India's National Association of Software and Service Companies) and the Indian authorities to change laws overnight so that call center staffers could work from home. Other laws had to be tweaked so that TCS workers could take laptops and other equipment out of physical offices located in India's "special economic zones." Irfhan Rawji, the founder and CEO of MobSquad, had to work closely with the Canadian government to ensure that the economic migrants chosen by the company to move to Canada could receive their expedited work permits and be integrated into its model. Any all-remote organization thinking about hiring talent globally has to consider local labor laws as they relate to hiring, compensation, pensions, vacation, and sick leave.

Is This Right for Your Organization?

Of course, WFA may not be possible at this time for some organizations, such as manufacturing companies—though that could change with advances in 3D printing, automation, digital twins, and other technologies. However, with the right strategy, organizational processes, technologies, and—most important—leadership, many more companies, teams, and functions than one might have thought could go all or mostly remote. My ongoing research with Jan Bena and David Rowat suggests, for example, that startup knowledge-work companies, particularly in the tech sector, are well positioned to adopt a WFA model from their inception. Take the all-remote eXp Realty: We found that lower real estate, utility, and other overhead costs may mean a higher valuation for the company if and when its founders exit the startup.

My studies of the USPTO and TCS indicate that large and mature organizations, too, can successfully transition to a hybrid or a majority-remote regime. The question is not whether work from anywhere is possible but what is needed to make it possible. The short answer: management. "If all senior leaders are working from an office, then workers would be drawn to that location to get face time," one all-remote middle manager told me. But if leaders support synchronous and asynchronous communication, brainstorming, and problem-solving; lead initiatives to codify knowledge online; encourage virtual socialization, team building, and mentoring; invest in and enforce data security; work with government stakeholders to ensure regulatory compliance; and set an example by becoming WFA employees themselves, all-remote organizations may indeed emerge as the future of work.

The pandemic has hastened a rise in remote working for knowledge-based organizations. Research into work-from-anywhere (WFA) organizations and groups can help leaders decide whether remote work is right for their organizations.

✓ WFA has notable benefits: Companies can save on real estate costs, hire and utilize talent globally, mitigate immigration issues, and experience productivity gains, while workers can enjoy geographic flexibility.

✓ Concerns about WFA include how to communicate across time zones, share knowledge that isn't yet codified, socialize virtually and prevent professional isolation, protect client data, and evaluate performance.

✓ If leaders support synchronous and asynchronous communication, lead initiatives to codify knowledge online, encourage virtual socialization, invest in and enforce data security, work with government stakeholders to ensure regulatory compliance, and set an example by becoming WFA employees themselves, all-remote organizations may indeed emerge as the future of work.

NOTES

1. Ravi S. Gajendran and David A. Harrison, “The Good, the Bad, and the Unknown About Telecommuting: Meta-analysis of Psychological Mediators and Individual Consequences,” *Journal of Applied Psychology* 92, no. 6 (2007): 1524–1541.

2. Nicholas A. Bloom et al., “Does Working from Home Work? Evidence from a Chinese Experiment,” *Quarterly Journal of Economics* 130, no. 1 (February 2015): 165–218.

3. Prithwiraj Choudhury, Cirrus Foroughi, and Barbara Larson, “Work-from-Anywhere: The Productivity Effects of Geographic Flexibility,” Harvard Business School Technology and Operations Mgt. Unit working paper no. 19-054 (August 7, 2019), https://papers.ssrn.com/sol3/papers.cfm?abstract_id=3494473.

4. Robin Cowan, Paul A. David, and Dominique Foray, “The Explicit Economics of Knowledge Codification and Tacitness,” *Industrial and Corporate Change* 9, no. 2 (1999): 211–253.

5. Cecily D. Cooper and Nancy B. Kurland, “Telecommuting, Professional Isolation, and Employee Development in Public and Private Organizations,” *Journal of Organizational Behavior* (April 2002): 511–532.

Adapted from an article in Harvard Business Review, *November–December 2020 (product #R2006C).*

2

TALK ABOUT MENTAL HEALTH WITH YOUR EMPLOYEES—WITHOUT OVERSTEPPING

by Deborah Grayson Riegel

It's been called a "second pandemic"—the mental health implications of the global health crisis, political unrest, economic uncertainty, rising unemployment, social isolation, remote work, homeschooling, and so much more.[1] And while it can feel like the first pandemic has been with us long enough for employees to have accessed the necessary resources and strategies for handling their stress, the fact is, many of us are struggling more, not less.

Talking about mental health can feel tricky at best and terrifying at worst, however. And it becomes a vicious cycle—the less people talk about it at work (even when they know they and others are struggling), the more the stigma grows. To break this cycle, you have to address the issue proactively, strategically, and thoughtfully. After all, the way we talk to others who are dealing with anxiety (and to ourselves) has a major impact on how we feel.

Managers have a responsibility to their employees to create an open, inclusive, and safe environment that allows them to bring their whole selves to work. In her article "We Need to Talk More About Mental Health at Work," Morra Aarons-Mele shares research showing that "feeling authentic and open at work leads to better performance, engagement, employee retention, and overall well-being."

Leaders at all levels need to put mental health "on the table"—to talk about it, invite others to talk about it, and work actively to develop resources and plans for their employees. This is how to reduce mental health stigma while increasing the likelihood that your colleagues feel happier, more confident, and more productive.

So how do you start talking about a topic that can make even the bravest leader worry about overstepping? Here are three ways:

Talk about health holistically

Chances are that you'd ask your coworker about the back pain they've been experiencing since they started working from home. You'd probably also ask your team member about the tendon they tore on a recent run. You might even share an update about your seasonal allergies or your indigestion. When you're asking about someone's health, make a note to ask about their mental health too. It can be as simple as, "It sounds like your back pain is getting better. That's good news. And how's your mental health these days? I know these can be very stressful times—and please let me know if I'm overstepping." (And then stop talking.)

It's helpful if you are willing to share your own struggles, too, because it normalizes the discussion. You might try, "My allergies are keeping me up at night—and so is my anxiety. It's really hard to get a solid night's sleep when I'm worried about my kids' safety at school. How about you? What's keeping you up at night?" (And then again, stop talking.) It's important to note that if you haven't had a close connection with a particular employee in the past, your query may feel intrusive or unsafe. To build up a psychologically safe relationship, take small steps. You might say something like, "I know that you and I haven't typically talked about nonwork topics, but for me, work and nonwork feel like they're blurring together these days. How are you doing with that?"

Don't try to fix people

Leaders often succeed by navigating difficult situations and solving complex problems. But people don't like to be "fixed," so don't try. An employee who believes you see them as broken may worry that you don't see them as capable or credible, which can undermine their confidence and competence. Approach your colleagues with the mindset that they are resourceful and able, and offer support rather than solutions. You want to be a *bridge* to resources, rather than being the resource yourself.

If someone shares that they are struggling, try saying:

- "What would be most helpful to you right now?"
- "What can I take off your plate?"

- “How can I support you without overstepping?”
- “Let’s discuss the resources we have available here and what else you might need.”
- “I’ve been through something similar. And while I don’t want to make this about me, I’m open to sharing my experience with you if and when it would be helpful.”

Really listen

Financier Bernard Baruch said, “Most of the successful people I’ve known are the ones who do more listening than talking.” But it’s not enough to just listen; you need to do it *well.* But that’s not always easy—especially now when our own preoccupations, distractions, biases, and judgments get in the way.

If you want to create an environment where your employees feel heard, respected, and cared for, here’s how:

- Be clear with yourself and your colleague that your intention for listening is to help.
- Suspend judgment (of yourself and the other person) by noticing when an “approving/disapproving”

thought enters your mind. Let it pass or actively send it away.

- Focus on your colleague and their experience, being sure to separate their experience from yours.
- Listen for overall themes, such as social isolation or financial concerns, and don't get mired in the details, which can distract you from the big picture of what's going on with them. Since you're there to support them, rather than solve their problems, you don't need to know the specifics.
- Listen with your eyes as well as your ears. Notice changes in facial expressions, which can give you some cues to what the person is actually feeling—and may be different from what they're saying.
- Recognize that when you start thinking to yourself, "What am I supposed to do?" you've stopped listening.
- Let your colleague know if something is interfering with your ability to really listen, whether it's an urgent email, your child demanding your attention, or your own stress—and offer to reschedule your conversation for a time when you can fully attend to them.

As World Health Organization ambassador Liya Kebede said, "Helping others isn't a chore; it is one of the greatest gifts there is." Your willingness to open an honest conversation about mental health with your employees is exactly the kind of gift that so many people want and need right now.

Leaders at all levels need to put mental health "on the table"—to talk about it, invite others to talk about it, and work actively to develop resources and plans for their employees.

- ✓ To the start the conversation, you should use physical health as a transition into talking about mental health, avoid making your employees feel like they are "broken," and actively listen.
- ✓ If you haven't had a close connection with a particular employee in the past, your relationship may be low on psychological safety. To start building that up, take small steps.

- ✓ It's not your job to be your employees' therapist, but it is your role to create an open, inclusive, and safe environment that allows them to bring their whole selves to work.

NOTE

1. Kristen R. Choi, MarySue V. Heilemann, and Alex Fauer, "A Second Pandemic: Mental Health Spillover from the Novel Coronavirus (Covid-19)," *Journal of the American Psychiatric Nurses Association* 26, no. 4 (July 2020): 340–343.

Adapted from "Talking About Mental Health with Your Employees—Without Overstepping" on hbr.org, November 3, 2020 (product #H05YOA).

3

WHY YOUR VALUES BELONG AT WORK

by Bea Boccalandro

About 20 years ago, I was a ski patroller. One afternoon I found myself halfway up a mountain attending to Dave, a man in his forties with an injured knee. As I positioned Dave in the sled that I would ski down to the clinic, he hurled obscenities. It wasn't because of his pain: My offense was being a woman.

I whispered to the male patroller who was assisting me: "Tom, since Dave is uncomfortable having a woman ski the sled down, should you do it instead?" Tom responded in a voice loud enough for Dave to hear. "On the contrary. Dave's objections are baseless. Your competent sled running might help him develop proper respect for women."

The events of 2020 deepened our awareness that people are routinely victims of prejudice, violence, lack of health-care access, and other forms of injustice because of their gender, race, country of origin, religion, sexual orientation, age, mental illness, physical limitations, and countless other factors. Many of us feel the pull to promote social justice and other societal causes, but we still have to dedicate most of our waking hours to our day jobs. But what if we seek ways to bring activism into our daily interactions at work? This tactic, which I call "job purposing," involves adjusting how we work so that we engage in social purpose, or a meaningful contribution to a societal cause, during the workweek. With his response to Dave's sexist comments, Tom deliberately brought activism into a work interaction. He job purposed.

The Many Benefits of Job Purposing

Most of us would consider Tom's pursuit of social purpose noble. We might be surprised to hear, though, that acts of workplace social purpose don't typically undermine success at work—they actually *promote* career success. Research finds that, compared to colleagues who don't job purpose, those who do likely have higher job satisfaction and performance, and they may even be happier and healthier.

It boosts job satisfaction

My research documented 13% higher job satisfaction, on average, in employees whose work experience incorporated social purpose than in those whose work didn't.[1] Other studies reached similar conclusions. For example, the Happiness Research Institute and Krifa in Denmark found that lack of workplace purpose is the biggest culprit in job dissatisfaction among Danes. Another European study found that incorporating social purpose into work boosted job satisfaction within two months.[2] In fact, so many studies link social purpose to job satisfaction that researchers who systematically reviewed all the evidence say the relationship is indisputable.[3]

It boosts performance

One experiment studied workers scanning online images for specific patterns. Members of a randomly selected subgroup were told that they were labeling tumor cells to assist medical researchers. The others were not given any context about the work. Workers who knew they were supporting the health of others processed more images—while maintaining the same level of quality—than those who had no reason to believe their work promoted social purpose.[4] Another study found that workers who knew they were pursuing social purpose were 24% faster and had 43% less downtime than those who didn't, and there was no loss of quality.[5]

The positive effect that job purposing has on work appears to add up to a more successful career. Studies find that job purposing is associated with a 10% higher likelihood of receiving a raise and a 40% higher likelihood of being promoted.[6]

It makes us calmer

Brain imaging reveals that acts of social purpose reduce the stress response at the cellular level.[7] Another study found that pursuing social purpose lowers the negative health impact of stressful situations like final exams and financial woes.[8]

It makes us healthier

Researchers randomly divided 73 older individuals suffering from high blood pressure into two groups. One group was given $120 and instructed to spend $40 on themselves every week for three weeks. Members of the other group were also given $120 but were asked to spend $40 on others every week. At the completion of the experiment, the self-oriented spenders had no change in blood pressure, yet the social-purpose spenders experienced a blood pressure drop as large as medication or exercise would have generated.[9] In another study, researchers randomly divided a group of adolescents into two groups; one volunteered for charitable causes and the other did not. Four months later, those who volunteered had lower cholesterol than those who hadn't.[10]

It makes us happier

Pursuing social purpose activates the same pleasure-producing area of the brain that sex and dessert do. Studies confirm the existence of this "helper's high" across genders, age, and other demographics.[11]

How Employees Are Job Purposing

Workers at every level of an organization can make co-worker and customer interactions more human, meetings more meaningful, operations more inclusive, and marketing more charitable. Employees at Bank of America, Disney, FedEx, PwC, Toyota, Western Digital, and other brands I've advised have done just that.

Many companies have adopted policies aimed at reducing bias and combating racism. For example, Starbucks and Walmart don't ask job applicants about criminal history to ensure their preliminary selection process doesn't discriminate against former felons, and plenty of HR departments and supervisors have rolled out unconscious-bias training to help identify patterns of discriminatory thinking and behavior. While these policies are important, smaller, individual actions can go a long way toward promoting social justice, too. Consider these real-world examples of individual job purposing:

- A supervisor at a *Fortune* 500 hospitality company consistently asks those who are quiet in meetings—who, evidence shows, are disproportionately women and people of color—to share their thoughts.

- A white realtor has preemptive conversations about unconscious bias with property owners before they review applications or offers. She explains that most people unknowingly view minority candidates less favorably than others, shares that it takes concerted effort to overcome this unconscious bias, urges them to make that effort, and provides links to resources to help them do so.

- A catering business orders at least 20% of its food from small businesses run by people from minority groups.

- A line worker at a manufacturing plant adopts a no-racism policy in conversations. If a coworker belittles any race, he says, "That's not cool. I won't take part in racism." If this doesn't stop the offenders, he leaves the conversation.

We can also leverage our day jobs to support other societal causes—including strengthening local nonprofits and helping victims of domestic violence—like these workers did:

- An instructor at an accounting firm replaced a written case study assignment in her new-hire class with free consulting for a local nonprofit. Now she strengthens nonprofit organizations through every training.

- After several clients dropped hints that they were victims of domestic violence, a hairdresser trained to become a victim advocate and now knows she's offering the type of response that's most likely to help.
- A commercial landlord loaned her vacant properties to a nonprofit that used them as staging areas for monthlong neighborhood cleanups.

About a year after I transported Dave down the mountain, I found him waiting for me at ski-patrol headquarters, where he apologized to me for his sexist remarks. It appears that Tom had nudged Dave toward being less prejudiced. That's the best part of job purposing—we can end our workweek gratified to know that we not only helped our organization but that we also made a positive societal impact.

It can feel hard to make a real, positive impact in your community when you spend so much of your time at work. Job purposing is a way to adjust how you work so that you make a meaningful contribution to a societal cause during the workweek.

- ✓ Job purposing involves adjusting how we work so that we engage in social purpose, or a meaningful contribution to a societal cause, while working.
- ✓ Ample research shows that job purposing boosts job satisfaction and performance and makes us calmer, healthier, and happier.
- ✓ Workers at every level of an organization can find creative ways to promote social justice and aid their communities while at work. For example, a catering business orders at least 20% of its food from small businesses run by people from minority groups.

NOTES

1. Joseph Chancellor, Seth Margolis, Katherine Jacobs Bao, and Sonja Lyubomirsky, "Everyday Prosociality in the Workplace: The Reinforcing Benefits of Giving, Getting, and Glimpsing," *Emotion* 18, no. 4 (June 2018): 507–517.

2. Ibid.

3. Blake A. Allan, Cassondra Batz-Barbarich, Haley M. Sterling, and Louis Tay, "Outcomes of Meaningful Work: A Meta-Analysis," *Journal of Management Studies* 56, no. 3 (May 2019): 500–528.

4. Dana Chandler and Adam Kapelner, "Breaking Monotony with Meaning: Motivation in Crowdsourcing Markets," *Journal of Economic Behavior and Organization* 90 (June 2013): 123–133.

5. Daniel Hedblom, Brent R. Hickman, and John A. List, "Toward an Understanding of Corporate Social Responsibility: Theory and Field Experimental Evidence," National Bureau Economic Research working paper no. 26222 (September 2019), https://www.nber.org/papers/w26222.

6. "Meaning and Purpose at Work," BetterUp, https://get.betterup.co/rs/600-WTC-654/images/betterup-meaning-purpose-at-work.pdf; Shawn Achor, "Positive Intelligence," *Harvard Business Review* (January–February 2012): 100–102.

7. Tristen K. Inagaki, Kate E. Bryne Haltom, Shosuke Suzuki, Ivana Jevtic, Erica Hornstein, Julienne E. Bower, and Naomi I. Eisenberger, "The Neurobiology of Giving Versus Receiving Support: The Role of Stress-Related and Social Reward–Related Neural Activity," *Psychosomatic Medicine* 78, no. 4 (May 2016): 443–453.

8. Michael J. Poulin and E. Alison Holman, "Helping Hands, Healthy Body? Oxytocin Receptor Gene and Prosocial Behavior Interact to Buffer the Association Between Stress and Physical Health," *Hormonal Behavior* 63, no. 3 (March 2013): 510–517.

9. Ashley V. Whillans, Elizabeth W. Dunn, Gillian M. Sandstrom, Sally S. Dickerson, Kenneth M. Madden, "Is Spending Money on Others Good for Your Heart?" *Health Psychology* 35, no. 6 (June 2016): 574–583.

10. Hannah M. C. Schreier, Kimberly A. Schonert-Reichl, and Edith Chen, "Effect of Volunteering on Risk Factors for Cardiovascular Disease in Adolescents: A Randomized Controlled Trial," *JAMA Pediatrics* 167, no. 4 (April 2013): 327–332.

11. Oliver Scott Curry, Lee A. Rowland, Caspar J. Van Lissa, Sally Zlotowitz, John Mcalaney, and Harvey Whitehouse, "Happy to Help? A Systematic Review and Meta-analysis of the Effects of Performing Acts of Kindness on the Well-Being of the Actor," *Journal of Experimental Social Psychology* 76 (March 2018): 320–329.

Adapted from content posted on hbr.org, January 21, 2021 (product #H063VX).

Section 2

THE NEW WORKFORCE

RETHINKING THE ON-DEMAND WORKFORCE

by Joseph Fuller, Manjari Raman, Allison Bailey, and Nithya Vaduganathan

In this era of chronic skills shortages, rapid automation, and digital transformation, companies are confronting a growing talent problem, one that has the potential to become a strategic bottleneck. How can they find people with the right skills to do the right work at just the right time? The half-life of skills is shrinking fast, and many jobs now come and go in a matter of years. Not only that, but major demographic changes are under way: boomers are aging out of the workforce, and millennials and Gen Z are taking over, bringing with them very different priorities about who should do what work—and where, when, and how it should get done.

To help companies address these challenges, a new generation of talent platforms—such as Catalant, InnoCentive, Kaggle, Toptal, and Upwork—has emerged. In contrast to Uber, Amazon Mechanical Turk, and TaskRabbit, these platforms offer on-demand access to *highly skilled* workers, and our research shows that their number has risen substantially since 2009, from roughly 80 to more than 330. Much of that growth took place during the past five years alone. Today almost all *Fortune* 500 companies use one or more of them.

Platforms that provide workers who have four-year college degrees or advanced degrees represent an increasingly important but understudied element of the emerging gig economy. To better understand this phenomenon, we undertook a survey of nearly 700 U.S. businesses that use them. We then conducted in-depth interviews with many corporate leaders whose companies are relying on the platforms and with platform founders and executives.

That companies are leveraging high-skills platforms in large numbers came as no surprise to us, because in recent years we've seen how they can increase labor force

---

Some of the companies mentioned in this article are clients of the Boston Consulting Group.

flexibility, accelerate time to market, and enable innovation. We were impressed, however, by the variety of engagements that companies are making with the platforms. They're seeking help with projects that are short- and long-term, tactical and strategic, specialized and general. What's more, 90% of the leaders we surveyed—C-suite and frontline—believe these platforms will be central to their ability to compete in the future.

But here's what did surprise us: Despite the extent to which companies are now turning to such platforms, very few firms have developed a cohesive organization-wide approach to their use. Instead, operational frontline leaders who are desperate to get things done have been reaching out to them on an ad hoc basis, often without any central guidance. This approach is costly, inefficient, and opaque.

To compete in the years ahead, companies must do better. They'll have to acknowledge and embrace the full potential of digital talent platforms—which is to say, figure out how to engage strategically with what you might call the *on-demand workforce.*

Though millions of workers were laid off this past spring, in the coming months employers will begin to rehire—and when they do, they'll need to be more purposeful about their approach to talent. How can they access hard-to-find expertise? Which positions or roles have changed, and what new capabilities are required? What work can be done more successfully and efficiently by skilled freelancers? In an environment of ongoing uncertainty, employers will be even more attracted to the freelance route for a variety of reasons: It makes hiring easier for hard-to-fill jobs, offers access to a wider set of skills, reduces head count, and allows more flexibility during times of change.

In this article we'll take stock of where most companies now stand on this front. We'll show how some pioneers are speeding ahead to take advantage of what the new talent platforms have to offer, and we'll explain how you and your management team can do the same.

The Maturing Gig Ecosystem

As the gig economy has grown, three kinds of platforms have emerged:

Marketplaces for premium talent

These platforms, which include Toptal and Catalant, allow companies to easily source high-end niche experts—anybody from big-data scientists to strategic project managers and even interim CEOs and CFOs. Toptal, for example, claims it culls the "top 3%" of freelancers from across the globe. Experts might be hired for strategic initiatives or embedded in teams, and the projects they're assigned to can range in length from a few hours to more than a year. The Covid-19 crisis is increasingly turning companies toward this kind of platform: Consider that this past spring Catalant reported a 250% increase in demand for supply-chain expertise. (Full disclosure: Coauthor Joseph Fuller is an adviser to Catalant's board of directors.)

Marketplaces for freelance workers

These platforms, which include Upwork, Freelancer, and 99designs, match individuals with companies for discrete task-oriented projects—designing a logo, say, or translating a legal document. For example, when Amazon wanted to explore creating custom social-media content for its new TV shows, it tested the waters with Tongal, which connects companies to individuals with media know-how. Many freelance platforms offer access to workers from around the world with a wide variety of skills, and payment is often per completed task. Covid-19 is accelerating the move toward these platforms, too:

As large swaths of society began working remotely, Upwork saw a spike in demand for digital marketing expertise from companies trying to reach consumers in their homes.

Platforms for crowdsourcing innovation

These platforms, which include InnoCentive and Kaggle, allow companies to post problems in large communities of technically sophisticated users—and reach a far broader base of them than could ever be found or developed in-house. The challenges run the gamut from simple coding projects to complex engineering dilemmas. Working with the platforms, companies often create competitions and offer prizes for the best solutions. The U.S. Transportation Security Administration, for example, ran a $1.5 million competition on Kaggle to help improve the algorithms that predict threats using images from airport scanning equipment. Enel, the Italian multinational energy company, uses multiple crowdsourcing platforms to generate ideas for a host of issues: how to improve recruiting and even what to do with defunct thermal plants. And the pharmaceutical company AstraZeneca has turned to InnoCentive's "solvers" to develop molecules used in genetic research and testing.

The Growing Supply

Millions of well-qualified Americans today are attracted to contract work. Freelancers are now estimated to make up roughly a third of the U.S. workforce, and those who are highly skilled represent a small but growing slice of it. And for the first time since 2014, the number of freelancers who say they consider gig work to be a long-term career choice is the same as the number who consider it a temporary way to make money. Early signs suggest that Covid-19 will also speed up this shift.

Much of the shift is the result of demographic changes that have been underway for four or five decades but that traditional organizations have done little to recognize or address. There are at least four key trends:

Care responsibilities

Single-parent and sandwich-generation families are on the rise. Burdened with childcare and eldercare, many employees are dropping out of the workforce or struggling to manage full-time jobs. Gigs allow them the flexibility to handle their family obligations while delivering quality work.

Female employment

Women's participation in the U.S. labor force has been declining steadily since 2000. Highly skilled, experienced women who take time off to have children and for other life events are finding it difficult to restart their careers or are seeing themselves get sidetracked in traditional organizations. According to a 2009 Center for Work-Life Policy survey, more than two-thirds of "highly qualified" women—that is, those with advanced degrees or high-honors BAs—who drop out of the workforce would not have done so if they'd had access to more-flexible job arrangements. Online talent platforms allow them to more smoothly reenter the workforce and advance their careers.

The aging of America

Workers who are laid off or edged out of traditional firms once they hit their fifties often find that talent platforms offer them a way to continue to use their skills and experience—while maintaining satisfying work/life balance. Given that by 2030 one in five Americans will be older than 65, talent platforms expect that experienced workers with hard-to-find skills will flock to their fold.

The millennial ascendancy

Millennials, who are already the largest generational cohort in the workforce, tend to be tech-savvy and to prefer to work for themselves rather than for traditional organizations. They want more autonomy and control over their job security than previous generations had.

Early Lessons

We've identified three areas where companies have consistently found talent platforms most useful:

Labor force flexibility

When the head of technology at the PGA, Kevin Scott, found himself frustrated by the need to constantly improve and upgrade the organization's digital capabilities and offerings despite a lack of in-house digital talent, he partnered with Upwork to quickly engage software engineers to generate and develop promising ideas. Using Upwork, the PGA was able to get projects started and finished considerably faster than before.

Time to market

Many managers have turned to talent platforms to fast-track processes, meet deliverables, and ensure outcomes. When Anheuser-Busch InBev wanted to quickly expand into new, disruptive products, it realized that despite having a workforce of 150,000, it needed outside help. By tapping into Catalant, the company was able to rapidly get consumer data analyzed and find experts to help roll out products like kombucha tea and spiked seltzer. Similarly, when Matt Collier, a senior director at Prudential PLC, was on a tight deadline to overhaul the training given to insurance agents in Singapore, he turned to Toptal to find designers and other talent that could help him create course materials quickly—and ended up getting the job done for less than it would have cost with traditional vendors.

Business model innovation

Digital talent platforms can also help companies reinvent the way they deliver value. In 2015, when Enel made the strategic choice to embrace the United Nations' 2030 sustainable development goals and build new businesses around them, it engaged the services of several crowd-sourcing platforms, among them InnoCentive, which alone gave Enel access to more than 400,000 of its highly skilled problem-solvers worldwide.

Overcoming Resistance

In our survey, C-suite executives in particular seemed to envision a future reliance on talent platforms: Half thought it "highly possible" that their core workforce (permanent full-time employees) would be much smaller in the years to come, and two-thirds told us they expected to increasingly "rent," "borrow," or "share" talent to meet specialized needs.

Why, then, have so few companies designed strategic approaches to working with talent platforms? Because the structures and processes that most organizations have in place have been designed expressly to protect them from external vendors, much as white blood cells protect our bodies from pathogens. If companies want to work successfully with digital platforms, they need new structures and processes that function as immunosuppressants.

That's a major change, and many vice presidents and directors are worried about the practical implications of embracing it. Integrating an on-demand workforce into a firm's strategic core, they recognize, means questioning and redesigning every aspect of the organization. For managers already in the throes of a digital transformation, the prospect of taking on another massive project is hardly appealing.

But a digital transformation requires a talent transformation. The two go hand in hand. Company leaders understand this. Nearly two-thirds of our survey respondents reported that "understanding the digital skills needed for the future" had been a top priority for them in the previous three years. The very nature of work changes with more technology and automation, as does a company's ability to find the skills needed to do that work. Online talent platforms provide a way to develop that ability rapidly and with much less effort.

Engineering the Talent Transformation

To engage with the on-demand workforce at a strategic level, companies will need to focus on five main challenges:

Reshaping the culture

When a company decides to turn core functions over to freelance workers, permanent employees often feel threatened. They struggle with sharing information, raise doubts about the values and work habits of outsiders, and assume the worst. That's what happened when NASA began using crowdsourcing platforms to generate innovative ideas: The organization's engineers began to worry about their job security and question their professional identities. As one employee put it, his colleagues were not used to saying, "Hey, we have a problem and we don't know how to solve it. Can you help?"

Often, the strongest opposition comes from employees who have the least exposure to high-skills talent platforms. The members of Enel's leadership team saw this when they decided to seek external innovation help. Pushback came not just from the rank and file but also from senior leaders who were nervous about the message this approach would send. Was turning to freelancers a sign of weakness? Did it signal that the leadership team lacked confidence in the permanent staff? But with some careful attention to cultural change, the company managed to overcome that resistance. Instead of allowing employees to fear the unknown, Enel focused on educating employees about how they could benefit from an on-demand workforce. According to Ernesto Ciorra, the company's chief "innovability" officer, the first step was to help all full-timers understand that they could use talent platforms to tap a powerful new source of strength. (*Innovability* is Enel's term for innovation plus sustainability.) "We had to become humbler," Ciorra told us, noting how important it was to recognize that at times "the best ideas lay outside the company."

Rethinking the employee value proposition

Companies need to get employees to see how they personally can benefit from talent platforms. That's what one private equity firm did when it rolled out plans to collaborate with Upwork. According to Hayden Brown, Upwork's CEO, the message the firm sent its employees was: "This is a way to help you. There are a lot of things that you may be doing in your day-to-day work that you can offload so that you can do even higher-order work or free yourself up to do more strategic thinking."

However, as more teams include full-time and gig employees, working norms will have to change. Full-time employees will often need to step into coach and "connector" roles—asking questions of outside colleagues, identifying discrete pieces of work for external partners, and making it possible for gig workers to tap institutional knowledge. Full-time and gig employees will also have to learn how to work productively across dispersed, often remote teams. They'll have to become adept at collaborating with a revolving set of teammates, articulating previously tacit team norms, and making progress easy for everybody to track. Companies will have to base promotion incentives for managers on outcomes attained rather than full-time employees overseen. Some talent platforms have already created tools—available through their enterprise agreements—that can help companies with these sorts of transitions.

Reorganizing work into components

One of the biggest predictors of whether a company will get the most out of a talent-platform partnership is how well it can break work down into rigorously defined components that can be easily handed over to outsiders. Most companies haven't focused on this, because in traditional workplaces, managers can afford to be vague when making assignments. They know that everybody on the project team will be interacting so frequently that they'll be able to clarify goals and make course corrections over time. But when companies use talent platforms, they have to provide much more up-front definition. Enel learned this lesson quickly when it adopted its open-innovation approach. As Ciorra told us, "You can't just say, 'I need something useful for my renewable-energy problem.' Instead, you have to be specific: 'I need to reduce the usage of *X* when I do *Y* in *Z* context.'" Only after employees started providing this kind of clarity in crowdsourcing appeals did the company begin getting the help it needed.

Reassessing capabilities

To engage strategically with talent platforms, companies need to develop a portfolio approach to skills. The first step is to understand which capabilities they have in-house, of course. Unilever uses the services of a company called Degreed, which allows employees to develop and certify their expertise in specific areas with so-called microcredentials. The employees get recognition for their know-how and understand exactly which skills they need to acquire to advance; the company benefits because it can now identify which skills the organization already has and who possesses them.

Once the company has mapped internal capabilities, it can prepare for step two: striking the right balance when dividing work up internally and externally. That's something Royal Dutch Shell tackled after identifying an urgent need to generate new revenue through digital and services growth. Using a cloud-based platform called Opportunity Hub that it already had in place, Shell was quickly able to assess the areas where it had the talent to speed toward its strategic goals and where it lacked the right skills. Soon it realized that it had shortfalls in key areas such as digitization and the internet of things—and that it didn't have the time to find and hire the right people. To get working immediately on projects in these areas, Shell partnered with Catalant.

Rewiring organizational policies and processes

This can be surprisingly difficult, as Collier discovered when he tried to bring in Toptal to help Prudential revamp thousands of training slides. A new mindset and a different way of working were necessary. "To adapt our initial contract for freelancers," Collier told us, "we had to navigate a number of necessary processes, including due diligence, intellectual property, technology risk, antibribery, even anti-money-laundering." To get the talent he urgently needed, Collier positioned working with Toptal as an experiment and persuaded stakeholders to give it a try. That paid off. Today, Prudential has a standard service agreement with the platform, and Collier readily leverages it for design and other types of skilled work.

A major challenge for companies that want to harness the on-demand workforce is that they're still subject to regulations and practices that evolved in the predigital era. At Unilever, for example, one struggle was figuring out how to pay freelancers from digital platforms. According to Adfer Muzaffar, a former Unilever senior manager for talent and learning, "Freelancers are accustomed to immediate payment on the platforms via a credit card. But we had longer payment terms, and credit card payment was not an option. We wanted to be able to track who we paid, what we were paying for, what was the quality of work, whether the rates offered were competitive compared to our local costs. So we had to find solutions so that our internal mechanisms and processes could support this new way of working."

Talent transformations are often easier than they might seem. That's because many companies have people on staff who already have a wealth of experience with talent platforms—the managers who have used them on an ad hoc basis. These people can provide valuable guidance.

Ultimately, however, to bring about change on the scale needed to innovate business models, companies will have to appoint a leader to explore how online workforce platforms can unlock new sources of value. This has to be somebody from the C-suite. It might be the CTO, the CMO, the CFO, or the CHRO—we've seen successful examples of each.

In the end, of course, it's not titles that matter. It's finding leaders who understand their companies' strategic positioning, who recognize the revolutionary potential of engaging with the on-demand workforce, and who can inspire a cultural shift in their organizations that will make a genuine transformation possible.

As companies struggle with chronic skills shortages and changing labor demographics, a new generation of talent platforms, offering on-demand access to highly trained workers, has begun to help. Almost all *Fortune* 500 firms use such platforms. But most do so in an ad hoc, inefficient way. To engage with the on-demand workforce at a strategic level, companies will need to:

- ✓ Make sure permanent employees don't feel threatened. Organizations can start by explaining how the platforms can personally benefit permanent employees.
- ✓ Understand which capabilities they have in-house, so they strike the right balance when dividing work up internally and externally.
- ✓ Adopt a new mindset and a different way of working. For example, organizations will need to update regulations and practices that evolved in the predigital era.
- ✓ Appoint a leader who understands their companies' strategic positioning and is committed to exploring how online workforce platforms can unlock new sources of value.

Adapted from an article in Harvard Business Review, *November–December 2020 (product #R2006G).*

5

A BETTER WAY TO ONBOARD AI

by Boris Babic, Daniel L. Chen, Theodoros Evgeniou, and Anne-Laure Fayard

In a 2018 Workforce Institute survey of 3,000 managers across eight industrialized nations, the majority of respondents described artificial intelligence as a valuable productivity tool.

It's easy to see why: AI brings tangible benefits in processing speed, accuracy, and consistency (machines don't make mistakes because they're tired), which is why many professionals now rely on it. Some medical specialists, for example, use AI tools to help make diagnoses and decisions about treatment.

But respondents to that survey also expressed fears that AI would take their jobs. They are not alone. The *Guardian* recently reported that more than six million workers in the United Kingdom fear being replaced by machines. These fears are echoed by academics and executives we meet at conferences and seminars. AI's advantages can be cast in a much darker light: Why would humans be needed when machines can do a better job?

The prevalence of such fears suggests that organizations looking to reap the benefits of AI need to be careful when introducing it to the people expected to work with it. Andrew Wilson, Accenture's CIO until January 2020, says, "The greater the degree of organizational focus on people helping AI and AI helping people, the greater the value achieved." Accenture has found that when companies make it clear that they are using AI to help people rather than to replace them, they significantly outperform companies that don't set that objective (or are unclear about their AI goals) along most dimensions of managerial productivity—notably speed, scalability, and effectiveness of decision making.

In other words, just as when new talent joins a team, AI must be set up to succeed rather than to fail.

Theodoros Evgeniou is an adviser to Marble Bar Asset Management (an investment firm named in this article).

A smart employer trains new hires by giving them simple tasks that build hands-on experience in a noncritical context and assigns them mentors to offer help and advice. This allows the newcomers to learn while others focus on higher-value tasks. As they gain experience and demonstrate that they can do the job, their mentors increasingly rely on them as sounding boards and entrust them with more-substantive decisions. Over time an apprentice becomes a partner, contributing skills and insight.

We believe this approach can work for artificial intelligence as well. In the following pages we draw on our own and others' research and consulting on AI and information systems implementation, along with organizational studies of innovation and work practices, to present a four-phase approach to implementing AI. It allows enterprises to cultivate people's trust—a key condition for adoption—and to work toward a distributed human-AI cognitive system in which people and AI *both* continually improve. Many organizations have experimented with phase 1, and some have progressed to phases 2 and 3. For now, phase 4 may be mostly a "future-casting" exercise of which we see some early signs, but it is feasible from a technological perspective and would provide more value to companies as they engage with artificial intelligence.

Phase 1: The Assistant

This first phase of onboarding artificial intelligence is rather like the process of training an assistant. You teach the new employee a few fundamental rules and hand over some basic but time-consuming tasks you normally do (such as filing online forms or summarizing documents), which frees you to focus on more-important aspects of the job. The trainee learns by watching you, performing the tasks, and asking questions.

One common task for AI assistants is sorting data. An example is the recommendation systems companies have used since the mid-1990s to help customers filter thousands of products and find the ones most relevant to them—Amazon and Netflix being among the leaders in this technology.

More and more business decisions now require this type of data sorting. When, for example, portfolio managers (PMs) are choosing stocks in which to invest, the information available is far more than a human can feasibly process, and new information comes out all the time, adding to the historical record. Software can make the task more manageable by immediately filtering stocks to meet predefined investment criteria. Natural-language processing, meanwhile, can identify the news most relevant to a company and even assess the general sentiment about an upcoming corporate event as reflected in analysts' reports. Marble Bar Asset Management (MBAM), a London-based investment firm founded in 2002, is an early convert to using such technologies in the workplace. It has developed a state-of-the-art platform, called RAID (Research Analysis & Information Database), to help PMs filter through high volumes of information about corporate events, news developments, and stock movements.

Another way AI can lend assistance is to model what a human might do. As anyone who uses Google will have noticed, prompts appear as a search phrase is typed in. Predictive text on a smartphone offers a similar way to speed up the process of typing. This kind of user modeling, related to what is sometimes called *judgmental bootstrapping*, was developed more than 30 years ago; it can easily be applied to decision making. AI would use it to identify the choice an employee is most likely to make, given that employee's past choices, and would suggest that choice as a starting point when the employee is faced with multiple decisions—speeding up, rather than actually doing, the job.

Let's look at this in a specific context. When airline employees are deciding how much food and drink to put on a given flight, they fill out catering orders, which involve a certain amount of calculation together with assumptions based on their experience of previous flights. Making the wrong choices incurs costs: Underordering risks upsetting customers who may avoid future travel on the airline. Overordering means the excess food will go to waste, and the plane will have increased its fuel consumption unnecessarily.

An algorithm can be very helpful in this context. AI can predict what the airline's catering manager would order by analyzing their past choices or using rules set by the manager. This "autocomplete" of "recommended orders" can be customized for every flight using all relevant historical data, including food and drink consumption on the route in question and even past purchasing behavior by passengers on the manifest for that flight. But as with predictive typing, human users can freely overwrite as needed; they are always in the driver's seat. AI simply assists them by imitating or anticipating their decision style.

It should not be a stretch for managers to work with AI in this way. We already do so in our personal lives, when we allow the autocomplete function to prefill forms for us online. In the workplace a manager can, for example, define specific rules for an AI assistant to follow when completing forms. In fact, many software tools currently used in the workplace (such as credit-rating programs) are already just that: collections of human-defined decision rules. The AI assistant can refine the rules by codifying the circumstances under which the manager actually follows them. This learning needn't involve any change in the manager's behavior, let alone any effort to "teach" the assistant.

Phase 2: The Monitor

The next step is to set up the AI system to provide real-time feedback. Thanks to machine-learning programs, AI can be trained to accurately forecast what a user's decision would be in a given situation (absent lapses in rationality owing to, for example, overconfidence or fatigue). If a user is about to make a choice that is inconsistent with their choice history, the system can flag the discrepancy. This is especially helpful during high-volume decision making, when human employees may be tired or distracted.

Research in psychology, behavioral economics, and cognitive science shows that humans have limited and imperfect reasoning capabilities, especially when it comes to statistical and probabilistic problems, which are ubiquitous in business. Several studies (of which one of us,

Chen, is a coauthor) concerning legal decisions found that judges grant political asylum more frequently before lunch than after, that they give lighter prison sentences if their NFL team won the previous day than if it lost, and that they will go easier on a defendant on the latter's birthday. Clearly justice might be better served if human decision makers were assisted by software that told them when a decision they were planning to make was inconsistent with their prior conclusion or with the choice that an analysis of purely legal variables would predict.

AI can deliver that kind of input. Another study (also with Chen as a coauthor) showed that AI programs processing a model made up of basic legal variables (constructed by the study's authors) can predict asylum decisions with roughly 80% accuracy on the date a case opens. The authors have added learning functionality to the program, which enables it to simulate the decision making of an individual judge by drawing on that judge's past decisions.

The approach translates well to other contexts. For example, when portfolio managers at Marble Bar Asset Management consider buy or sell decisions that may raise the overall portfolio risk—for example, by increasing exposure to a particular sector or geography—the system alerts them through a pop-up during a computerized transaction process so that they can adjust appropriately. A PM may ignore such feedback as long as company risk limits are observed. But, in any case, the feedback helps the PM reflect on their decisions.

Of course, AI is not always “right.” Often its suggestions don’t take into account some reliable private information to which the human decision maker has access, so the AI might steer an employee off course rather than simply correct for possible behavioral biases. That’s why using it should be like a dialogue, in which the algorithm provides nudges according to the data it has while the human teaches the AI by explaining why they overrode a particular nudge. This improves the AI’s usefulness and preserves the autonomy of the human decision maker.

Unfortunately, many AI systems are set up to usurp that autonomy. Once an algorithm has flagged a bank transaction as possibly fraudulent, for example, employees are often unable to approve the transaction without clearing it with a supervisor or even an outside auditor. Sometimes undoing a machine’s choice is next to impossible—a persistent source of frustration for both customers and customer-service professionals. In many cases the rationale for an AI choice is opaque, and employees are in no position to question that choice even when mistakes have been made.

Privacy is another big issue when machines collect data on the decisions people make. In addition to giving humans control in their exchanges with AI, we need to guarantee that any data it collects on them is kept confidential. A wall ought to separate the engineering team from management; otherwise employees may worry that if they freely interact with the system and make mistakes, they might later suffer for them.

Also, companies should set rules about designing and interacting with AI to ensure organizational consistency in norms and practices. These rules might specify the level of predictive accuracy required to show a nudge or to offer a reason for one; criteria for the necessity of a nudge; and the conditions under which an employee should either follow the AI's instruction or refer it to a superior rather than accept or reject it.

To help employees retain their sense of control in phase 2, we advise managers and systems designers to involve them in design: Engage them as experts to define the data that will be used and to determine ground truth; familiarize them with models during development; and provide training and interaction as those models are deployed. In the process, employees will see how the models are built, how the data is managed, and why the machines make the recommendations they do.

When AI Loses Its Way

In 2016 the investigative newsroom ProPublica published an exposé of a risk-prediction AI program known as COMPAS, which judges in southern Florida use to determine a defendant's likelihood of reoffending within a specified time period.

The algorithm underlying COMPAS is held as a trade secret by its manufacturer, Northpointe (now Equivant), which means that we don't know how COMPAS generates its predictions, nor do we have access to the data the algorithm is trained on—so we cannot even inquire into its rationale. When it was reported that the algorithm produces disparate outcomes across race, COMPAS immediately became a leading example of why people cannot trust AI.

If businesses want employees to adopt, use, and ultimately trust AI systems, it will be important to open up the black box—to the extent legally possible—to those who are expected to engage with the technology. As Richard Socher, the chief scientist at Salesforce, put it, "If businesses use AI to make predictions, they owe humans an explanation as to how the decisions are made."

Phase 3: The Coach

In a recent PwC survey nearly 60% of respondents said that they would like to get performance feedback on a daily or a weekly basis. It's not hard to see why. As Peter Drucker asserted in his famous 2005 *Harvard Business Review* article "Managing Oneself," people generally don't know what they are good at. And when they think they do know, they are usually wrong.

The trouble is that the only way to discover strengths and opportunities for improvement is through a careful analysis of key decisions and actions. That requires documenting expectations about outcomes and then, nine months to a year later, comparing those expectations with what actually happened. Thus the feedback employees get usually comes from hierarchical superiors during a review—not at a time or in a format of the recipient's choosing. That is unfortunate, because, as Tessa West of New York University found in a recent neuroscience study, the more people feel that their autonomy is protected and that they are in control of the conversation—able to choose, for example, when feedback is given—the better they respond to it.[1]

AI could address this problem. The capabilities we've already mentioned could easily generate feedback for employees, enabling them to look at their own performance and reflect on variations and errors. A monthly summary analyzing data drawn from their past behavior might help them better understand their decision patterns and practices. A few companies, notably in the financial sector, are taking this approach. Portfolio managers at MBAM, for example, receive feedback from a data analytics system that captures investment decisions at the individual level.

The data can reveal interesting and varying biases among PMs. Some may be more loss-averse than others, holding on to underperforming investments longer than they should. Others may be overconfident, possibly taking on too large a position in a given investment. The analysis identifies these behaviors and—like a coach—provides personalized feedback that highlights behavioral changes over time, suggesting how to improve decisions. But it is up to the PMs to decide how to incorporate the feedback. MBAM's leadership believes this "trading enhancement" is becoming a core differentiator that both helps develop PMs and makes the organization more attractive.

What's more, just as a good mentor learns from the insights of the people who are being mentored, a machine-learning "coachbot" learns from the decisions of an empowered human employee. In the relationship we've described, a human can disagree with the coachbot—and that creates new data that will change the AI's implicit model. For example, if a PM decides not to trade a highlighted stock because of recent company events, they can provide an explanation to the system. With this feedback, the data that the system continually captures can be analyzed to provide more useful insights.

If employees can relate to and control exchanges with artificial intelligence, they are more likely to see it as a safe channel for feedback that aims to help rather than to assess performance. Choosing the right interface is useful to this end. At MBAM, for example, trading enhancement tools—visuals, for instance—are personalized to reflect a PM's preferences.

As in phase 2, involving employees in designing the system is essential. When AI is a coach, people will be even more fearful of disempowerment. A coachbot can easily seem like a competitor rather than a partner—and who wants to feel less intelligent than a machine? Concerns about autonomy and privacy may be even stronger. Working with a coach requires honesty, and people may hesitate to be open with one that might share unflattering data with the folks in HR.

Deploying AI in the ways described in the first three phases does of course have some downsides. Over the long term, new technologies create more jobs than they destroy, but meanwhile labor markets may be painfully disrupted. What's more, as Matt Beane argues in "Learning to Work with Intelligent Machines" (HBR, September–October 2019), companies that deploy AI can leave employees with fewer opportunities for hands-on learning and mentorship.

There is some risk, therefore, not only of losing entry-level jobs (because digital assistants can effectively replace human ones) but also of compromising the ability of future decision makers to think for themselves. That's not inevitable, however. As Beane suggests, companies could use their artificial intelligence to create different and better learning opportunities for their employees while improving the system by making it more transparent and giving employees more control. Because future entrants to the workforce will have grown up in a human-plus-machine workplace, they will almost certainly be faster than their pre-AI colleagues at spotting opportunities to innovate and introduce activities that add value and create jobs—which brings us to the final phase.

Phase 4: The Teammate

Edwin Hutchins, a cognitive anthropologist, developed what is known as the theory of distributed cognition. It is based on his study of ship navigation, which, he showed, involved a combination of sailors, charts, rulers, compasses, and a plotting tool. The theory broadly relates to the concept of extended mind, which posits that cognitive processing, and associated mental acts such as belief and intention, are not necessarily limited to the brain, or even the body. External tools and instruments can, under the right conditions, play a role in cognitive processing and create what is known as a *coupled system.*

In line with this thinking, in the final phase of the AI implementation journey (which to our knowledge no organization has yet adopted) companies would develop a coupled network of humans and machines in which both contribute expertise. We believe that as AI improves through its interactions with individual users, analyzing and even modeling expert users by drawing on data about their past decisions and behaviors, a community of experts (humans and machines) will naturally emerge in organizations that have fully integrated AI coachbots. For example, a purchasing manager who—with one click at the moment of decision—could see what price someone else would give could benefit from a customized collective of experts.

Although the technology to create this kind of collective intelligence now exists, this phase is fraught with challenges. For example, any such integration of AI must avoid building in old or new biases and must respect human privacy concerns so that people can trust the AI as much as they would a human partner. That in itself is a pretty big challenge, given the volume of research demonstrating how hard it is to build trust among humans.

The best approaches to building trust in the workplace rely on the relationship between trust and understanding—a subject of study by David Danks and colleagues at Carnegie Mellon. According to this model, I trust someone because I understand that person's values, desires, and intentions, and they demonstrate that they have my best interests at heart. Although understanding has historically been a basis for building trust in human relationships, it is potentially well suited to cultivating human-AI partnerships as well, because employees' fear of artificial intelligence is usually grounded in a lack of understanding of how AI works.

In building understanding, a particular challenge is defining what "explanation" means—let alone "good explanation." This challenge is the focus of a lot of research. For example, one of us (Evgeniou) is working to open up machine-learning "black boxes" by means of so-called counterfactual explanations. A counterfactual explanation illuminates a particular decision of an AI system (for example, to approve credit for a given transaction) by identifying a short list of transaction characteristics that drove the decision one way or another. Had any of the characteristics been different (or counter to the fact), the system would have made a different decision (credit would have been denied).

Evgeniou is also exploring what people perceive as good explanations for AI decisions. For example, do they see an explanation as better when it's presented in terms of a logical combination of features ("The transaction was approved because it had XYZ characteristics") or when it's presented relative to other decisions ("The transaction was approved because it looks like other approved transactions, and here they are for you to see")? As research into what makes AI explainable continues, AI systems should become more transparent, thus facilitating trust.

Conclusion

Adopting new technologies has always been a major challenge—and the more impact a technology has, the bigger the challenge. Because of its potential impact, artificial intelligence may be perceived as particularly difficult to implement. Yet if done mindfully, adoption can be fairly smooth. That is precisely why companies must ensure that AI's design and development are responsible—especially with regard to transparency, decision autonomy, and privacy—and that it engages the people who will be working with it. Otherwise they will quite reasonably fear being constrained—or even replaced—by machines that are making all sorts of decisions in ways they don't understand.

Getting past these fears to create a trusting relationship with AI is key. In all four phases described in these pages, humans determine the ground rules. With a responsible design, AI may become a true partner in the workplace—rapidly processing large volumes of varied data in a consistent manner to enhance the intuition and creativity of humans, who in turn teach the machine.

AI's advantages can be cast in a dark light: Many ask why humans would be needed when machines can do a better job. Organizations looking to reap the benefits of AI need to be careful introducing it to the people expected to work with it.

- ✓ Employers must set AI up to succeed rather than to fail. Companies should ensure that AI's design and development are responsible and that it engages the people who will be working with it.

- ✓ Successful implementation can be broken down into a four-phase approach: train the AI system, set up the AI to provide real-time feedback, introduce the AI as a coach, and finally, as a teammate.
- ✓ The four-phase approach helps cultivate people's trust and works toward a distributed cognitive system in which humans and AI both continually improve.

NOTE

1. David Rock, Chris Jones, and Beth Weller, "Using Neuroscience to Make Feedback Work and Feel Better," *Strategy + Business* 93 (August 2018), https://www.strategy-business.com/article/Using-Neuroscience-to-Make-Feedback-Work-and-Feel-Better?gko=6aca6.

Adapted from an article in Harvard Business Review, *July–August 2020 (product #R2004C).*

Section 3

REDEFINING THE INCLUSIVE ORGANIZATION

6

"WOKE-WASHING" YOUR COMPANY WON'T CUT IT

by Erin Dowell and Marlette Jackson

Kelli, a data scientist at a tech company, recently submitted a request for a promotion. Her responsibilities had increased after turnover on her team, and she felt the extra work merited recognition. But she was told that the VP who needed to approve the promotion didn't have time to consider it—they were too preoccupied crafting a company response to the renewed conversations about racial injustice and police brutality. As a Black woman asking for her work to be recognized, she was struck by the hypocrisy. "I found it ironic that senior leadership prioritized their public image when internally they dismissed or ignored the very Black voices that they claimed to care about," she told us. "It made the gesture of solidarity feel like a slap in the face."

As companies all over the United States have rushed to advertise their commitment to racial justice and claim common cause with a historic protest movement, we've seen a lot of stories like Kelli's. Her sentiments are representative of the many employees experiencing statement fatigue—a growing level of disinterest, ambivalence, and outright outrage toward companies calling out racial injustice without showing any signs of taking action. And in the current U.S. social climate, employees are becoming more empowered to call out their company's hypocrisy—juxtaposing solidarity statements with lopsided statistics of company representation and personal accounts of negative workplace experiences.

While many companies are speaking out because they know the costs of silence are high, they're discovering that the costs of "woke-washing"—appropriating the language of social activism into marketing materials, for instance—can be high, too. Organizations such as Whole Foods, Pinterest, and Adidas have all seen public complaints from current and former employees that corporate statements of solidarity glossed over internal inequities. For many workers, such statements from executive leadership underscore how the same leaders who rally for Black lives have fallen short when it comes to addressing these problems. Empty company statements can seem to say that Black lives only matter to big business when there's profit to be made.

As diversity, equity, and inclusion practitioners, scholars, and consultants, we have firsthand experience navigating these challenges in the workplace. In our work, we investigate acts of discrimination, facilitate workshops on cultural competency and social justice, render institutional policy advice, consult with leaders on diversity issues, and mediate diversity-centered conflict. But more than this, as Black women, we share the professional and personal toll current events are having on communities of color. Accordingly, we recognize the importance of moving beyond solidarity statements and toward power dynamics that effectively eradicate the underlying anti-Blackness that has been central to America's origin story and thus, the American corporate story.

We'll tell you right now: While statements of solidarity are a starting point, we are at a critical juncture as a nation and the moment demands more. Diversity and inclusion efforts, on a collision course with the Black Lives Matter movement, have jointly arrived at the corporate table demanding justice. But how, exactly, can companies show that they're committed to just change? They can start by (1) prioritizing and assessing corporate accountability, (2) committing to corporate structural evolution, and (3) realigning the power dynamic between the organization and its employees, providing employees more agency to drive company culture. To assist organizations in this time of transition, we've put together a blueprint for corporate social justice—a playbook of what executives can do to foster anti-racism at the organizational, leadership, and individual level.

Organizational Accountability: Create a Data-Driven Action Plan

Because many corporate solidarity statements focus on operational change at the organizational level, it's necessary to first discuss what accountability should look like in the social justice context. When articulating next steps, organizations must consider that this accountability is multifaceted. We draw here from the work of Alnoor Ebrahim, professor of management in the Fletcher School of Law and Diplomacy, who focuses on the accountability challenges faced by organizations of various types. Professor Ebrahim provides four tenets that are highly applicable to mapping next steps for organizational accountability:[1]

- **Transparency.** As companies determine what their social justice course of action should look like, transparency regarding the details and the outcome are essential for winning employee trust. Start by engaging in diligent research to identify how your company's social justice goals can be met and making these findings available for review. This fact-finding can be achieved via surveys or focus groups conducted among employees or by partnering with community organizations or consultants to render this insight. This qualitative data will serve as the foundation of a new relationship between the C-suite and employees—a critical dynamic in the push for organizational social justice—and ensure that employee voices, particularly Black employee voices, are heard on the cultural issues impeding organizational social justice. This open process makes room for a more inclusive environment with meaningful data at its core.
- **Justification.** It's essential that an action-oriented plan provide clear reasons for why the company is taking the specific next steps it is to advance corporate social justice. This justification should include research-based support for options the organization will pursue, as well as those the

organization has declined to explore further. Again, relying on the data here makes this a much easier task.

- **Compliance.** After an organization has moved from solidarity statements to an action plan, it will be necessary to monitor and evaluate implementation of that plan. While this can be achieved via an oversight committee or task force, it is important to also enact checks and balances to mitigate the effects of bureaucracy on the action plan's progress. Organizations should build on each of these accountability tenets while moving through the process—transparency and justification should remain hallmarks of the compliance process.

- **Enforcement.** After rolling out an employee-vetted action plan, organizations must prepare for and respond to areas in which compliance will inevitably miss the mark. Transparency is paramount here, and continued commitment to dialogue—especially in the face of shortfalls—is the key to an ultimate realignment of the power dynamic between employees and the corporation at large. At the conclusion of this process, organizations should emerge with at least two things that will prove infinitely more valuable than an initial statement of solidarity: a data-driven progress report detailing its path toward social justice and a trust-driven employee culture of inclusion.

Concrete and tangible strategies that may result from an employee-vetted action plan include: (1) ensuring manager performance reviews assess whether leaders are cultivating a culture of equity and inclusion, (2) cocreating with and financially supporting community partners on local social justice initiatives, (3) recognizing employee acts of service (employee resource groups, diversity recruitment) in performance evaluations, (4) providing intersectional social justice programming, and (5) mitigating structures that amplify privilege with tools such as blind résumés and skill-based hiring tests, as well as the elimination of salary history questions, low entry-level pay, inadequate benefits, unpaid internships, and educational prerequisites that do not align with job responsibilities.

Accountability in Leadership: Change Starts at the Top

A commitment to corporate structural evolution means that executive leadership must be willing to change the way in which the organization works. This includes looking for diverse faces in nontraditional spaces—in particular, expanding the roles of individuals beyond "chief diversity presence." However, accountability in leadership must also bring a shift in the balance of power at the top of organizations, and a reframing of the ways that power is wielded.

Black leaders are critical voices in the conversation about the current state of accountability and organizational justice. We asked three experts from our network (and are only using their first names so they can speak candidly) for their take. From their perspectives, organizational accountability in leadership requires these three critical factors:

- **Be intentional about building your pipeline.** Dr. Terrence B., chief pharmacy officer at a family health center, suggests that companies "develop relationships with historically Black colleges and universities whose academic departments emphasize majors and skills relevant to that company's industry." Once a company has attracted talented Black recruits to its pool, Terrence recommends continuing this intentional commitment to developing Black leadership via internal programs that provide necessary training to promising employees.

- **Patronize Black businesses and promote internal Black talent.** "Externally, [companies] can patronize Black businesses and invest in Black entrepreneurs through exposure, acceleration, and contracts," says Danny A., vice president of tech diversity and inclusion at a *Fortune* 500 software company. "Internally, organizations should have people of color on their boards. The progression of Black employees typically gets them to supervisory roles but elevation to senior management is much less likely. It signals to Black employees that 'you can handle the base operations, but I don't want you in my boardroom.'" Danny notes the role that affinity bias plays in this trend, adding that often, executive leadership decides that "someone who looks like me is someone I think should be in this role."

- **Leverage your growing social justice tool kit to navigate the future.** Kristine M., a global operations professional at a major social network, notes that "companies attack areas of social injustice, diversity, and inclusion like a game of whack-a-mole—reactively addressing specific concerns as they come with no lasting impact." By optimizing the skills and resources discussed here, companies can be better positioned to think proactively in order to drive sustainable change.

Individual Accountability: Build In the Tools of Empowerment

To seed real change, it's essential to give employees the ability to drive institutional culture. Organizations must be cognizant of the forces accompanying each employee to work and afford them the space and tools to advance social justice from the bottom up.

- Psychological safety. Organizations should prioritize the psychological safety of employees. This must include ongoing initiatives such as robust counseling and support options, as well as a corporate willingness to remain open and attuned to the voices, needs, and challenges of employees. Larger companies may foot the bill to train culturally competent counselors and counselors from a range of backgrounds to address these needs, while smaller organizations may consider drafting memoranda of understanding with community organizations to provide comparable counseling resources.

- **Advocacy education.** Organizations should provide the educational foundation and tools for employees to learn the skills they need to operate as "active bystanders" for social justice, or how to engage in inclusive conversations. As with the formulation of a social justice action plan, organizations should review their cultural competency and diversity training curricula, soliciting feedback on what is truly working and what is ineffective. In a time where scholarship, technology, and creativity have produced a spectrum of resources from anti-racism books to apps, there is no limit to an organization's capacity to create a curriculum with the necessary social justice components.
- **Regular pulse checks.** Organizations should establish systems for regularly gauging the climate of inclusion. This practice may include surveys and follow-up connections with employees who can identify opportunities for improvement. These check-ins should be consistent without becoming so mundane that employees are no longer motivated to participate. Increase engagement by reporting on success and challenges of the social justice goals.

Fostering organizational justice will require a deep institutional commitment at the industrial, executive, and individual level. Organizations must be cognizant of the fact that the current outcry for justice is not ephemeral or confined to social media. It is the culmination of decades of advocacy and centuries of discrimination, and as such, consumers are no longer willing to let organizations squander those efforts.

Consumers not only hold the power of demand but are increasingly demonstrating that they also have a strong voice in deciding the manner in which companies meet those demands—and organizations need to be mindful of how this dynamic is becoming part of the new normal. By implementing the strategies laid out here, companies advance social justice by reprioritizing the voices of their employees, while soliciting a partnership for navigating the organization's future.

While statements of solidarity are a starting point in supporting racial justice, the moment demands more from organizations.

- ✓ Use transparency, justification, compliance, and enforcement as four tenets to consider your organization's social justice accountability and plan next steps.

- ✓ Executive leadership must be willing to change the way in which the organization works. Leadership must bring a shift in the balance of power at the top of organizations and a reframing of the ways that power is wielded.
- ✓ Give employees the ability to drive institutional culture. Organizations must be cognizant of the forces accompanying each employee to work and afford them the space and tools to advance social justice from the bottom up.

NOTE

1. Alnoor S. Ebrahim, "The Many Faces of Nonprofit Accountability," Harvard Business School working paper no. 10-069 (2010).

Adapted from content posted on hbr.org, July 27, 2020 (product #H05QM9).

7

ARE YOUR D&I EFFORTS HELPING EMPLOYEES FEEL LIKE THEY BELONG?

by Michael Slepian

Diversity brings many benefits to organizations—but it is not enough on its own. An organization with a diverse workforce is not necessarily an inclusive one. Diversity efforts now often fall under the banner of "diversity and inclusion" for this reason, but new research in a forthcoming issue of *Social Psychological and Personality Science* shows that inclusion may also fall short because it does not necessarily lead to a sense of *belonging.*[1]

Employees may feel they don't belong for any number of reasons, but in each case the result is the same: what researchers term an *identity threat*. Defined as any situation that makes salient that one is different from others, identity threats can range from trivial to troubling. Consider the manager who talks to her low-wage employees about upcoming international travel plans or the coworker who expresses surprise that a Black colleague doesn't conform to a stereotype. My colleague Drew Jacoby-Senghor and I set out to understand the impacts of identity-threatening situations like these that people experience on a regular basis.

We recruited 1,500 individuals who spanned a range of identities, including women working in male-dominated fields, people from multiple racial groups, LGBTQ-identifying individuals, as well as people with a range of ideologies, cultures, socioeconomic backgrounds, education levels, family environments, and current hardships. The extent of diversity that we examined is rare for research in the diversity space, which typically focuses on a limited set of identities and often one at a time. Instead, we examined experiences with identity threat that transcend specific identities and contexts, allowing us to make conclusions about diversity issues, in general, rather than just particular kinds of diversity.

We asked our participants whether they recently experienced identity-threatening situations, and they reported that they had many such experiences, an average of 11 in a week. When we probed further, we found that encountering identity-threatening situations was associated with feeling less included and also reduced belonging, but importantly these were two very different experiences. We found that across a very diverse set of identities and situations, a sense of exclusion was associated with negative emotion, but it was feeling like one did not belong that had a more pernicious effect. When employees felt like they didn't belong in the workplace, they felt like they couldn't be themselves at work. When employees feel they can't be their authentic self at work, they have lower workplace satisfaction, find less meaning in their work, and have one foot out the door.

With good reason, organizations often focus on inclusion in their diversity initiatives, but efforts toward inclusion that do not foster belonging can backfire. In a follow-up study, we asked employees about their interactions with their teammates and supervisors. Whether interacting with their teammates or their supervisor, our participants made a distinction between what we call real inclusion, versus surface inclusion.

When employees felt included, involved, and accepted (real inclusion), they felt like they belonged in the workplace. When employees felt like others asked for their input only because they were supposed to, or sought their opinion as someone who can represent their social group (surface inclusion), they felt like they belonged *less*. When being included for surface-level reasons, such as seeking a minority opinion, people can feel singled out on the basis of their demographics. This reduced sense of belonging works directly against inclusion efforts.

What can managers do? First, recognize but don't overemphasize differences. It is now clear that a color-blind approach does not effectively manage diversity in the workplace.[2] Color-blind policies can leave employees feeling ignored. On the other side of the spectrum, a multicultural approach that focuses on emphasizing and celebrating people's differences can too easily slide into unintentional endorsement of stereotypes and expectancies for specific differences between groups. Organizations must strike a middle ground that allows minority members to feel included while not feeling singled out. This middle ground recognizes that people want their social groups to be included in the conversation, but they do not want to be individually included solely on the basis of their category memberships.

Second, managers should focus on the creation of identity-safe environments.[3] Addressing underrepresentation at different leadership levels takes time, but managers today can focus on creating environments that demonstrate a value for individuals from underrepresented backgrounds and demographics. Managers should survey their employee's experiences to best understand what this should look like in their workplace, and how this might be implemented (for example, in a team-based core values exercise), but critically, the burden of this task must not be placed on minority members as this would only serve to single them out. What is acceptable behavior in the workplace? How can the organization speak to diverse audiences and consumers? Do not only look to minorities to answer these questions. Instead, include everyone in the conversation. The solution is to make *all* employees feel heard, and not single out only minority individuals, or expect them to always take the lead on diversity questions.

Third, feelings of support and being valued are critical.[4] Our study found that employees regarded organizational inclusion efforts as more surface level than real when they did not feel respected, valued, or supported by the organization. And so, it is important that employees feel that support systems are available to them at the broader organizational level. Leaders must create environments where employees feel comfortable speaking up when they see something that does not seem inclusive. Formal channels should allow employees to connect with leaders and mentors, and managers would be wise to listen to recommendations from HR and employee relations representatives for best practices when it comes to reporting concerns. Employees need to feel their concerns are heard, rather than dismissed or diminished.

Finally, the framing of inclusion attempts influences perceptions of sincerity. When it comes to the organization as a whole, inclusion should absolutely focus on different social groups and increasing representation. But when it comes to the day-to-day, inclusion efforts should be focused more on the individual than the social group they represent. Managers should include and reach out to employees from underrepresented backgrounds, but the framing of these appeals and communications is critical. Rather than treating an employee as a representative of people like them, instead consider their unique experiences and frame requests for input along these lines. Perhaps an employee has been in a different industry, has a unique job history, or currently has a project that requires unique forms of support.

The secret to making employees feel included is getting to know the people on your team as individuals.

A leftover vestige from color-blind approaches to diversity management is a tendency to value homogeny and to seek sameness. A team with a homogenous set of viewpoints will come to a decision smoothly, but often too smoothly, overemphasizing shared perspectives and overlooking critical details or opportunities for innovation. Sameness is not an asset. Learning about individuals' unique strengths and unique experiences, and openly recognizing them for these, is what leads employees to feel valued and respected. This is what enables going beyond surface-level inclusion in favor of real, individual-based inclusion. Inclusion efforts may be well meaning, but without a backbone of support and respect they may seem less than genuine.

People want their social group to be included and their individual self to belong. These are two different things. Managers can hit both targets when diversity initiatives do consider social identity, but inclusion initiatives focus on the individual. Managers should not only signal that a social identity is valued but also that the individual is valued, as a person, not just on the basis of the social group they represent. Support and recognition from coworkers, particularly those in leadership positions, foster feelings of inclusion *and* belonging.

A diverse workforce brings many benefits to organizations—but being diverse does not necessarily mean it is inclusive. And inclusion may fall short because it does not necessarily lead to a sense of *belonging*. What can managers do?

- ✓ Recognize but don't overemphasize differences. A color-blind approach does not effectively manage diversity in the workplace and can leave employees feeling ignored.
- ✓ Managers should focus on the creation of identity-safe environments.
- ✓ Leaders must create environments where employees feel comfortable speaking up when they see something that does not seem inclusive.
- ✓ While inclusion efforts should absolutely center on different social groups and increasing representation, these efforts should be focused more on the individual than on the social group they represent. This is the tightrope that leaders must walk.

NOTES

1. Michael L. Slepian and Drew S. Jacoby-Senghor, "Identity Threats in Everyday Life: Distinguishing Belonging from Inclusion," *Social Psychological and Personality Science* 12, no. 3 (2021): 392–406.

2. Adam D. Galinsky et al., "Maximizing the Gains and Minimizing the Pains of Diversity: A Policy Perspective," *Perspectives on Psychological Science* 10, no. 6 (November 2015): 742–748.

3. Colette Van Laar et al., "Coping with Stigma in the Workplace: Understanding the Role of Threat Regulation, Supportive Factors, and Potential Hidden Costs," *Frontiers in Psychology* 10 (August 2019), https://www.frontiersin.org/articles/10.3389/fpsyg.2019.01879/full.

4. Linda Rhoades and Robert Eisenberger, "Perceived Organizational Support: A Review of the Literature," *Journal of Applied Psychology* 87, no. 4 (August 2002): 698–714.

Adapted from content posted on hbr.org, August 19, 2020 (product #H05T6D).

Section 4

THE PURPOSE-DRIVEN ORGANIZATION

8

SOCIAL-IMPACT EFFORTS THAT CREATE REAL VALUE

by George Serafeim

Until the mid-2010s few investors paid attention to environmental, social, and governance (ESG) data—information about companies' carbon footprints, labor policies, board makeup, and so forth. Today the data is widely used by investors. Some screen out poor ESG performers, assuming that the factors that cause companies to receive low ESG ratings will result in weak financial results. Some seek out high ESG performers, expecting exemplary ESG behaviors to drive superior financial results, or wishing, for ethical reasons, to invest only in "green funds." Other investors incorporate ESG data into fundamental analysis. And some use the data as activists, investing and then urging companies to clean up their acts.

It's an open question whether ESG issues will remain as salient to investors during a global pandemic and the associated economic challenges—but my bet is that they will. That's because companies are likely to be more resilient in the face of unexpected shocks and hardships if they are managed for the long term and in line with societal megatrends, such as inclusion and climate change. Indeed, in the opening weeks of global bear markets following the spread of Covid-19, most ESG funds outperformed their benchmarks. And when colleagues and I looked at data for more than 3,000 firms between late February and late March 2020—when global financial markets were collapsing—we found that the ones the public perceived as behaving more responsibly had less-negative stock returns than their competitors. I believe that, longer term, the crisis is likely to increase awareness that companies must consider societal needs, not just short-term profits. The prominence of the Black Lives Matter movement, too, created a groundswell of support for strong diversity policies and fair employment practices. It seems clear that companies will be under growing pressure to improve their performance on ESG dimensions in the future.

The challenge for many corporate leaders is that they aren't sure how to do that. They lack understanding of exactly where they should be focusing their attention and how they should be communicating their ESG efforts. Many executives incorrectly believe that simple actions will suffice: improving ESG disclosures, releasing a sustainability report, or holding a sustainability-focused investor relations event. Some companies take those actions, fail to see a benefit, and grow disappointed or frustrated. In some cases they face criticism and negative reactions from investors.

It's easy to see why this has happened. Too many companies have embraced a "box-ticking" culture that encourages the adoption of increasingly standardized ESG activities, many of them created by analysts and consultants who rely on industry benchmarks and best practices. Those activities may well be good for society and the bottom line. Firms reap clear benefits in the form of operational efficiencies: After all, ESG measures such as reducing waste, strengthening relationships with external stakeholders, and improving risk management and compliance are good business hygiene. In many industries such efforts are now table stakes for enterprises wishing to remain competitive.

But they're not enough. Companies must move beyond box checking and window dressing. In a world that increasingly judges them on their ESG performance, they must look to more-fundamental drivers—particularly strategy—to achieve real results and be rewarded for them. Over the past two decades various colleagues and I have analyzed more than 10,000 companies, conducting 30 field studies and publishing more than 15 empirical papers. Our collective research points to the need for a new management paradigm for corporate leaders—one in which ESG considerations are embedded in both strategy and operations.

In this article I describe a five-pronged approach to help companies achieve superior performance through attention to environmental sustainability, social responsibility, and good governance. Pursuing this work isn't about ESG ratings per se—it's about using ESG integration to create new forms of competitive advantage. And since it involves fundamental strategic and operational choices, it can't be left entirely to the investor relations team or the sustainability department. Instead it must be a priority for the CEO and top executives and become central to the firm's culture.

Why ESG Issues Matter

The most fundamental reason to try to raise your company's ESG performance is that all human beings—in and out of corporate settings—have an obligation to behave in prosocial ways. But apart from the moral case, there are very real payoffs for focusing on ESG issues. And those extend beyond the benefits companies might enjoy because of productivity increases due to higher employee engagement or sales increases due to more loyal and satisfied customers.

First, an ESG focus can help management reduce capital costs and improve the firm's valuation. That's because as more investors look to put money into companies with stronger ESG performance, larger pools of capital will be available to those companies. My research colleagues and I have found this happening not only in equity markets but also in loan markets, where some banks are linking interest rates on loans to ESG performance. ING, for example, did just that in 2017 when it made a $1.2 billion loan to Philips, an innovator in health technology and consumer products.

Second, positive action and transparency on ESG matters can help companies protect their valuations as more global regulators and governments mandate ESG disclosures. My research with Jody Grewal of the University of Toronto and Edward Riedl of Boston University showed that after the European Union announced broader disclosure requirements, the stock market reacted positively to firms with strong ESG disclosure and negatively to those with weak disclosure. And it's not only developed countries that are adopting and enforcing disclosure regulations; so are many emerging markets, including South Africa, Brazil, India, and China.

Third, efforts to ensure sustainable practices will help maintain shareholder satisfaction with board leadership. As more investors with more assets under management commit to ESG investing, they will have more voting power to effect changes. Shareholders in a growing number of companies have already put forward proposals to improve gender diversity on the boards, garnering a level of support that was unimaginable even 10 years ago. For example, nearly 63% of voting shareholders at Cognex, a maker of machine vision products, approved a proposal to diversify the board, while a similar measure at the real estate company Hudson Pacific Properties received 85% support. To avoid votes against directors, challenges to executive-pay initiatives, and the like, management needs to be proactive about addressing ESG issues.

Finally, and perhaps most important, ESG practices are part of long-term strategy, and every company needs investors who support management's vision and plans for the future. When Paul Polman became the CEO of Unilever, then an underperforming consumer goods giant, he immediately ended quarterly earnings guidance and was explicit about his commitment to long-term strategy rather than short-term profits. That led to an exodus of short-term-focused investors, thereby attracting more-patient capital.

So how can companies get ahead of the trends and realize tangible financial benefits from their ESG programs? In my experience studying and advising companies with strong programs, I have identified five actions that management can take: Adopt strategic ESG practices; create accountability structures for ESG integration; identify a corporate purpose and build a culture around it; make operational changes to ensure that the ESG strategy is successfully executed; and commit to transparency and relationship-building with investors.

A Strategic ESG Program

To date, most companies have been treating ESG efforts like a cell phone case—something added for protection (in this case, protection of the firm's reputation). Corporate leaders need to replace this mentality with an ambitious and differentiated ESG strategy if they want to see real financial dividends.

In his seminal article "What Is Strategy?" (HBR, November–December 1996), Michael Porter draws a distinction between operational effectiveness and strategy. The former, he writes, "means performing similar activities better than rivals"; the latter "is about being different." Following Porter's distinction, an ESG program may deliver efficiencies and other operational improvements—maybe even some that are necessary for corporate survival—but it will boost long-term financial performance only if it provides strategic differentiation from competitors.

For example, some companies implement environmental-, water-, or waste-management systems in order to operate more efficiently. Although such systems would be included in ESG ratings, few if any companies would expect to establish a competitive advantage simply by adopting them. Typically, competitors can quickly follow suit and acquire similar systems. My research with Ioannis Ioannou of London Business School suggests that this is indeed what has happened. Analyzing data from close to 4,000 companies globally, we found that within most industries, ESG practices converged over the eight years from 2012 through 2019. In other words, firms are increasingly engaging in the same sorts of sustainability and governance activities—and thus failing to differentiate themselves strategically.

To outperform their competitors, companies need to find approaches that are more difficult to imitate. In our study we identified the ESG activities in each industry that have become widespread, which we termed *common* practices, and those that have not, which we termed *strategic*. As an example of the latter, think of Airbnb's creation of a peer-to-peer network and a "circular economy" business model (one involving the reuse of existing assets) or Google's unconventional approach to employee recruitment, engagement, and retention. Those distinctive practices have helped Airbnb and Google occupy competitive positions that cannot be easily replicated—and the companies have been rewarded by capital markets as a result. Indeed, our research confirms that the adoption of strategic ESG practices is significantly and positively associated with both return on capital and market valuation multiples, even after accounting for a firm's past financial performance.

So how can companies identify strategic ESG initiatives? As with any strategy, the way to start is by determining where to play and how to win. The former is particularly vital because not all ESG issues are created equal—some matter more, depending on the industry. In the energy and transportation sectors, for instance, investing to make the transition to a low-carbon economy is becoming increasingly important, affecting companies' costs and margins. In the technology sector, however, carbon-footprint reduction is not as relevant as building a diverse organization, which can bolster a brand's reputation and lead to increased revenue.

My research with Aaron Yoon of Northwestern University and Mozaffar Khan, a former colleague at HBS, has shown that targeting the right issues brings financial benefits: In analyzing the performance of more than 2,000 U.S. companies over 21 years, we found that those firms that improved on *material* ESG issues significantly outperformed their competitors. (Materiality was identified by the Sustainability Accounting Standards Board, or SASB, which offers a list of salient issues for 77 industries. I served as an unpaid member of SASB's Standards Council from 2012 to 2014.) Interestingly, companies that outperformed on *immaterial* ESG issues slightly underperformed their competitors. This suggests that investors are becoming sophisticated enough to tell the difference between greenwashing and value creation.

Of course, materiality is not a static concept. The strategic challenge for corporate leaders is to be foresighted about the ESG themes that are emerging as important industry drivers—to identify them before their competitors do (and in some cases ahead of SASB too). This requires leaders to conceptualize the various actors in the system, their incentives, and the interventions that could drive change. Although that may sound straightforward, it is not. But my research with Jean Rogers, the founder and former CEO of SASB, revealed that an ESG issue is likely to become financially material under certain conditions:

- When it becomes easier for management and external stakeholders to gain insight into a company's environmental or social impact (consider how technological advances now make it possible to trace the raw materials in electronic products and discern those that have been unsustainably mined)
- When the media and NGOs have more power and politicians are more responsive to it (such scenarios have prompted the creation and enforcement of anticorruption laws and other new regulations)
- When companies lack the ability to effectively self-regulate (for instance, in the case of the palm oil industry, where a misalignment of incentives for farmers lead to deforestation)
- When a company develops a differentiated service or product that replaces a "dirty" or unsustainable way of doing business (think of Tesla, with its potential to disrupt the market for gasoline-powered cars)

IKEA is one company that has mapped out a strategic ESG program, transforming itself in response to accelerating environmental degradation. It has introduced various product, service, and process innovations to move away from its traditional retailing of inexpensive furniture that customers often discard quickly. It recently entered the home solar and energy-storage business, which grew by 29% in 2019. And while most competitors are focusing on using materials more efficiently or trying to find ways to recycle products *after* they have been designed, IKEA has launched an effort to completely rethink product design. The aim is to create products that can be reused, refurbished, remanufactured, or recycled, thereby extending their life span. Moreover, IKEA products will be modularized to make them easy to dismantle and reuse as raw materials when they're no longer functional. Although this process will take years, the firm will most likely emerge as a circular-economy leader as more regulatory, consumer, and brand pressures force companies to compete on products with better environmental credentials.

While IKEA's strategy involves moving away from wasteful practices, other firms have found that strategic reviews can identify ways to differentiate by leaning in to positive impact. When senior leaders at Vaseline interviewed medical professionals at the Centers for Disease Control and Prevention, Doctors Without Borders, and the UN Refugee Agency, they learned that Vaseline jelly was an indispensable part of emergency first-aid kits, particularly in developing countries. They also learned that preventable skin conditions, such as deeply cracked hands and burns from cooking on gas stoves or using kerosene lamps, were keeping people from working, going to school, and engaging in other basic activities—a situation that Vaseline could help alleviate. That insight led to a new social-impact strategy to help heal the skin of five million people living in crisis or conflict. The strategy connected business goals with societal needs and differentiated the brand from competitors while increasing revenue.

Accountability Mechanisms

The implementation of an ESG strategy involves large operational and strategic changes. It must start at the top with the board and be diffused through the entire organization. Yet my research shows that in most companies the board of directors is far removed from the firm's ESG efforts. This is a mistake. The board should be the entity that ensures that ESG metrics are properly considered in executive compensation and are adequately measured and disclosed as part of the audit committee's work. Indeed, my colleagues and I have found that one of the characteristics of organizations with high ESG performance is a process that deeply embeds ESG issues in the board's work and in executive pay.

Although most large global companies say that their boards oversee sustainability, that generally happens in a piecemeal fashion. There are exceptions. BNP Paribas is a global financial company taking a systematic approach to sustainability governance. The company has directors who are active participants in sustainable-finance forums, including a chair who was formerly the president of the European Bank for Reconstruction and Development. Large polluters, such as BHP, Royal Dutch Shell, and Eskom, have linked executive incentives to their carbon emissions, motivating management to act as it faces increased risk of regulation and competition from new technologies. Microsoft and other technology firms have tied executive compensation to workforce diversity targets, an ESG issue that's critical for an industry in which competitiveness requires innovation, fresh ideas, and creative thinking.

The Power of Purpose

A top-down approach to sustainability and good governance is not effective if it is not supported from the bottom up by a culture that rallies around ESG initiatives. Many strategic efforts fail because people further down in the organizational hierarchy don't believe there is a true commitment to ESG goals or they lack clear direction for achieving them. Skepticism, even cynicism, leads such efforts to be sidelined or inconsistently implemented across functions, divisions, and business lines.

To remedy this problem, organizations must identify a corporate purpose and build a culture around it. When Claudine Gartenberg of the Wharton School, Andrea Prat of Columbia University, and I analyzed data from more than 1,000 U.S. companies and 1.5 million employees, we found that clarity about a sense of purpose declines from senior management to middle management and then to lower-level employees. We also found that firms able to flatten the hierarchy and diffuse a sense of purpose through the ranks outperformed their competitors.

In recent years a lot has been written about purpose, but not much consensus exists about what the term actually means. The most high-profile articulation of the concept came from Larry Fink, the CEO of BlackRock, the largest asset management firm in the world. He wrote that "a company cannot achieve long-term profits without embracing purpose" because "a strong sense of purpose and a commitment to stakeholders helps a company connect more deeply to its customers and adjust to the changing demands of society." In August 2019, CEOs from 181 of the world's largest companies—as part of the lobbying group Business Roundtable (BRT)—modified a position that the group had held since 1977 by declaring that the purpose of a corporation is not just to serve shareholders but to create value for all stakeholders.

Neither Fink's nor BRT's assertion explains exactly what purpose is, of course. But we definitely know what it is not: words you see on a wall when you enter company headquarters, mission statements posted on websites, or grandiose speeches by CEOs in town halls. Research has shown those to be "cheap talk" that is unrelated to real outcomes in the organization.

My colleagues and I have defined purpose as how employees—the people who know the organization best—perceive the meaning and impact of their work. To measure employees' sense of purpose in three of our recent studies, we used questions from surveys by the Great Place to Work Institute, asking participants to rate their level of agreement with statements such as: "My work has special meaning; it's not just a job," "I feel proud of the ways that we contribute to the community," and "Management has a clear view of where the organization is going and how to get there."

Investors seem to be paying increasing attention to companies that are effective at linking strategy to purpose. The Strategic Investor Initiative, an outgrowth of the Chief Executives for Corporate Purpose coalition, recently collaborated with KKS Advisors (which I co-founded) to analyze 20 CEO presentations on long-term strategic plans. We found that when CEOs did well at communicating corporate purpose, stock prices and trade volume rose in the following days. The implication is that investors find value in information about purpose. In one of the presentations we studied, Kenneth Frazier, the CEO of Merck, told shareholders: "Our purpose is very clear to us and all of our people, and that is to discover and develop lifesaving medicines for society." He added, "That's what makes our people come to work every day. It's what makes them make the tremendous commitment that gives them the willingness to make the discretionary effort."

For some companies, defining their purpose means leaving money on the table, at least in the short term. This is the case with automakers that are transitioning away from carbon-emitting gas-powered cars and moving toward electric vehicles, which are more eco-friendly but less profitable. The good news, though, is that we're seeing more examples proving that a long-term trade-off between profits and sustainability is not necessary, given that companies can redesign how they generate revenue. Consider Philips Lighting, which has shifted from selling light bulb products with limited life spans to selling lighting as a sustainable service. Customers pay for the light they use rather than investing in the physical assets, while Philips retains ownership of all lighting equipment and takes it back when it's suitable for recycling or upgrading.

Commitment to a purpose will also push companies to sometimes undertake initiatives that might not pencil out in P&L terms. Frazier described such an initiative when he spoke about Merck's effort to develop an Ebola vaccine: "It would have been impossible to say . . . 'We won't go there, because we don't see a robust commercial market.' And I think that's part of what [we are] talking about in terms of having a purpose-driven organization."

As more companies work to articulate their purpose and build a culture that fully embraces it, we will learn more about what ensures success. However, my research with Gartenberg already points to three key conditions: an intentional strategy to grow leaders within the organization, resulting in the promotion of internal candidates to the CEO role; fair compensation structures (in which the ratio of CEO pay to median worker pay is not extreme for the industry); and careful execution of mergers and acquisitions to avoid culture clashes. Though the reasons aren't fully understood, the research suggests that externally hired CEOs and companies with more acquisitions need to work harder to create a sense of purpose.

Operational Changes

In studying firms that have successfully implemented an ESG strategy, I've noticed that they tend to pass through three phases: efforts to reduce risk and ensure compliance with environmental regulations and other laws, efforts to improve operating efficiency, and efforts to innovate and grow. To achieve this evolution, exemplary firms usually start by centralizing ESG activities, which is helpful for moving from a focus on risk and compliance to a focus on operating efficiency. But to reach the innovation and growth stage, companies need to decentralize ESG activities and empower corporate functions to take responsibility for them. This is true in terms of distributing power from the C-suite to middle management, but it's also true at the board level. Initially a board needs to set up a separate sustainability committee. But at the third stage it will typically reallocate responsibilities to preexisting board committees (audit, nomination, and so forth).

Of course, decentralization requires appropriate support mechanisms. For example, the chemicals company

Solvay developed a tool to assess the environmental impact of each of its product applications. This has enabled decision makers in separate functions to take environmental considerations into account when discharging their respective responsibilities—for apportioning the R&D budget, underwriting risks during the due diligence phase of acquisitions, or optimizing plant manufacturing operations as regulations change. From 2016 to 2018 Solvay saw 4% annual growth in sales of products that have low environmental impact, while sales of more-damaging products declined by 5%.

As the ESG field continues to mature, investors will be looking at how organizations are structured to deliver on their stated purpose. To increase the odds of success, winning companies will make sure that the people who manage the most important determinants of ESG performance have the capabilities and resources needed to get the job done.

A first step is to ensure that the chief sustainability officer, or the senior executive charged with ESG responsibilities, is the person closest to the company's most material ESG issues. If brands are critical assets (as they are for consumer goods companies), this individual might be the chief marketing or chief brand officer. If risk management is a central concern for the enterprise (as is the case for financial institutions), this person could be the chief risk or chief investment officer. If human capital issues matter most, the responsibility for ESG activities might fall to the head of human resources. At Tyson Foods, the former chief sustainability officer also served as the executive vice president of corporate strategy and led continuous improvement efforts. In addition, he managed Tyson's venture fund, which is investing in plant-based protein and cultured meat as more-sustainable alternatives to traditional meat products.

Goal setting can be useful in helping companies progress from centralization to decentralization of ESG activities. Although top leaders should set ESG targets, unit heads and middle management should be empowered to figure out how to hit them. Paradoxically, audacious targets are more likely to be met than modest ones are. That was the finding that emerged when Ioannou and I, along with Shelley Xin Li of the University of Southern California, analyzed more than 800 corporate targets related to climate change. And a separate study—one I did with Grewal and my Harvard Business School colleague David Freiberg—confirmed the benefits of aiming high: We looked at more than 1,000 firms and discovered that those with relatively ambitious targets relating to climate change invested more than their peers, made significant operating changes, and, in the process, drove innovation.

Communicate with the (Right) Investors

Companies must avoid slavishly focusing on improving their ESG ratings, but communication with the investor community is nevertheless important. Often, however, decisions about what to measure and how to keep investors informed are clouded by misconceptions.

The first is the belief among many corporate leaders that a firm's investor base is not subject to influence or control by management. In reality, a company *can* influence who buys its stock and, if necessary, change the base of shareholders. It's not as easy as shaping one's customer or employee base, but it's possible. For example, before Shire was acquired by Takeda Pharmaceuticals, it significantly altered its investor base from 2006 to 2012 by committing to integrating financially material ESG issues into its strategy and reporting on them to its shareholders. Dedicated long-term investors (including Aviva Investors, Scottish Widows, and the Norwegian sovereign wealth fund) initially owned a small fraction of Shire's stock, but their holdings increased steadily and eventually became greater than those of transient investors—a highly uncommon phenomenon for a publicly listed company.

The second misconception is that the demands of sell-side analysts employed by big brokerage houses should determine what must be communicated. Most companies still emphasize mostly short-term information in their investor communications. That's because they view the sell side as the traditional "customer" of investor relations. That needs to change; the focus should be on communicating directly with the buy side—the large institutional asset managers that hold the company's stock.

The third misconception is that ESG metrics are sufficient for investors to integrate ESG considerations into their business analysis, valuation, and modeling. In fact, investors struggle to embed those metrics in financial models because it's not clear what they mean or how they can affect the financials. One solution might be the creation of a system of impact-weighted accounting that could measure a firm's environmental and social impacts (both positive and negative), convert them to monetary terms, and then reflect them in financial statements. Though the science to do this has yet to be perfected, such a system holds great promise for three reasons: It would translate impacts into units of measurement that business managers and investors understand; it would allow for the use of financial and business analysis tools to consider those impacts; and it would enable an aggregation and comparison of analyses across types of impact that would not be possible without standardized units of measurement.

At the Impact-Weighted Accounts Initiative (a Harvard Business School project that I lead), we are collaborating with the Global Steering Group for Impact Investing and the Impact Management Project on a simple approach: adjusting traditional accounting measures to consider the various types of impact that ESG actions might have. These include *product* impact, which affects revenue numbers; *employment* impact, which affects employee expenditures on the income statement; and *environmental* impact, which affects the cost of goods sold. For example, positive product impact could mean more revenue for a company and potentially higher growth. Positive employment impact (measured by, say, resources spent on employee training) would send investors a strong signal that management views employee expenditures as investments that lead to future profitability and not merely as expenses. Negative environmental impact might raise the cost of goods sold by triggering new and restrictive regulations.

Valuing a company's effects on people and the planet—and integrating that into traditional financial analysis—will offer a more comprehensive picture of actual corporate performance. Some companies, such as the science-oriented DSM and the pharmaceutical giant Novartis, are already experimenting with impact-weighted accounting. Novartis estimated its employment impact for 2017—including benefits derived from employee development, occupational safety efforts, and payment of a living wage—at $7 billion. Its environmental impact, as measured by carbon emissions and water and waste impacts, was calculated at $4.7 billion. Positive product impact, something that has been largely missing from most ESG investment frameworks, was estimated at $72 billion.

A final, fundamental misconception about investor relations is the idea that ESG disclosure is transaction-based and can happen intermittently. Companies need instead to see it as an opportunity for continual reputation and relationship building. It used to be that most communication with investors (the buy side) was happening through Wall Street analysts (the sell side). Increasingly, investors want a direct line of communication, and they appreciate proactive information sharing, which has the added benefit of extending investor patience. Performance declines may occur. But if CEOs come to investors with an excuse after the fact, without having built trust, they are unlikely to be given the leeway or the time they need to reverse the decline.

The Path Forward

Many companies have failed to recognize that the functional role of ESG data has changed over time. Initially such data was used to judge a company's willingness to avoid harm and do good. As a result, it was primarily an input to help form policies that signaled a firm's commitment to achieving positive outcomes for the environment and society.

However, investors are increasingly asking a different question: not whether a company has good intentions but whether it has the strategic vision and capabilities to achieve and maintain strong ESG performance. That means companies need to start measuring and reporting the results of their initiatives. Instead of communicating their *policies* for improving data privacy, water management, climate change mitigation, diversity, and other issues, they must communicate *outcome metrics* such as the number of customer accounts hacked, liters of water consumed per unit of product produced, carbon emissions saved, and percentage of women and people of color promoted internally to management positions.

Moving from intention to results is the next evolution that investors are looking for. The only way to outperform in this new era will be for companies to make material ESG issues central to their strategy and operations, to go above and beyond their competitors, and then to measure and communicate their superior performance. Global society faces enormous challenges. But if companies are bold and strategic with their ESG activities, they will be rewarded.

Companies don't win over investors just by issuing sustainability reports and engaging in other standard ESG practices. In a world that increasingly judges them on their ESG performance, they must look to more-fundamental drivers—particularly strategy—to achieve real results and be rewarded for them. Organizations should integrate ESG efforts into strategy and operations, and they should follow a five-pronged ESG approach to achieve superior performance:

- ✓ Identify the material issues in your industry, and develop initiatives that set your firm apart from rivals.

- ✓ Create accountability mechanisms to ensure your board's commitment.
- ✓ Infuse your whole organization with a sense of purpose and enthusiasm for sustainability and good governance.
- ✓ Decentralize ESG activities throughout your operations.
- ✓ Communicate regularly and transparently with your investors about ESG matters.

Adapted from an article in Harvard Business Review, *September–October 2020 (product #R2005B).*

9

COMPANIES MUST GO BEYOND RANDOM ACTS OF HUMANITARIANISM

by Frank Cooper III and Ranjay Gulati

Best Buy CEO Hubert Joly struck a note of optimism when he credited a number of companies for moving early to address the challenges of the Covid-19 pandemic and calling on others to "lead with purpose and humanity." The compassionate response of the business community was indeed impressive at a critical moment of crisis. But, as time has passed, people are calling for more than just random acts of humanitarianism. They want a sustained, thoughtful, and authentic response on the part of business, one that can deliver broader, long-term impact.

Many purpose-driven companies, from Best Buy to Facebook, have opted to provide outright grants for humanitarian efforts or have repurposed their manufacturing lines to produce needed health supplies, like hand sanitizer and ventilators. These measures are laudably altruistic, and they undoubtedly benefit communities, customers, and other stakeholders. They also, we should note, carry important reputational and motivational benefits, helping companies cultivate loyal customers and highly motivated employees.

And yet, such measures are limited in their impact and unsustainable, not least because companies in challenging times have limited budgets they can allocate to them. They also tend to lack authenticity, disconnected as they frequently are from core operations. Any organization can write a check or mobilize other resources. Corporate crisis response becomes much more meaningful when stakeholders know that the organization has been applying itself in similar ways and as part of its primary business over time for society's benefit, and that it will continue to do so far into the future.

When taken seriously, purpose provides a company with a concise and piercing definition of why it chooses to exist. It's an efficient way to unify employees, customers, suppliers, communities, and shareholders, creating an internal rallying cry and a framework to engage with the external world. It gives leaders the courage and conviction to navigate uncertainty and fear. The best way for a purpose-driven company to deliver aid during a crisis is to take inspiration and guidance directly from its reason for being. Make your efforts a clear extension not merely of what the company does, but *who* it is, and you can mobilize far more resources for impact while unifying stakeholders in the process.

During the pandemic, Microsoft has been living its purpose "to empower every person and every organization on the planet to achieve more" by partnering with UNICEF to create a remote learning platform to help the more than 1.5 billion students worldwide who have been affected by school closures. They've teamed up with Adaptive Biotechnologies to help analyze the virus's effects on the immune system. And they've created an open source code that pandemic researchers in the academic community can use. "Your core business model must be aligned with the world around you doing well," Microsoft chief executive, Satya Nadella, told *Fortune*. Never is that more important than during a crisis.

Mahindra Group, the Indian conglomerate, has long defined its purpose in a single word: "Rise." The idea is to strive for change that improves lives. One key way the company's financing arm, Mahindra Finance, has lived its purpose is by providing innovative financing to its core customers, residents of poverty-stricken rural areas of India. During the Covid-19 crisis, Mahindra, as a conglomerate, has devised many different ways to provide aid, from offering its resorts as health-care facilities to using its IT infrastructure to monitor virus outbreaks in cities. But it has also remained true to its investments in rural India, creating a fund to keep the economic and social backbone of those areas—its small businesses—afloat.

PayPal, the frictionless online payment system, has stated that its purpose is to "democratize financial services." In recent years, it has lived that purpose by providing business loans to entrepreneurs and small businesses, especially those that don't have access to other forms of capital. In response to the pandemic and its economic fallout, PayPal became one of the first nonbanks to offer Paycheck Protection Program loans. Doing this, of course, benefits the company, which gets the guaranteed interest from the government. But it also delivers on PayPal's purpose: The company has used its efficient platform to quickly get loans out to its customers (more than 10 million thus far), many of whom do not have access to bank financing. PayPal's customers, like Mahindra's, will likely remember these acts when the crisis has passed.

Rather than just doing good works in the name of purpose, let your purpose guide your response. Think deeply about what your company stands for and how you might best use that to confront the present circumstances. Think through the differential impact on disparate interests that each course of action might entail, and use your purpose as the compass to help guide you in choosing the right path. How might you best deliver on your reason for being, even if certain stakeholders don't benefit as much as others in the short term? If your business must make painful cuts, how might your purpose guide those decisions? Do any new opportunities exist to deliver value to society, even if a commercial logic doesn't yet exist? The best purpose-driven companies take a leap and pursue social benefits, having faith that they'll figure out a sustainable business model. Periods of crisis, when customer needs are fast evolving, can be fertile times for such experiments.

When a company and its leaders frame a reaction carefully and deliberately in line with their purpose, they will come out on the other side stronger, with supportive and united stakeholders and having delivered more positive impact. They show that the organization, through its core reason for being, will adapt to changing circumstances in the most principled of ways and be a force for good in the world. As Starbucks CEO Kevin Johnson remarked recently, "If we're not changed when we come out of this, we've missed an opportunity."

Any organization can write a check or mobilize resources when confronted with a crisis. But people are looking for more—a sustained, thoughtful, and authentic response on the part of business, one that can deliver broader, long-term impact.

- ✓ A well-defined organizational purpose should drive any actions you take. For example, PayPal has declared that it wants to democratize financial services, and it was one of the first nonbanks to offer Paycheck Protection Program loans.

- ✓ The best purpose-driven companies take a leap and pursue social benefits, having faith that they'll figure out a sustainable business model. Periods of crisis, when customer needs are fast evolving, can be fertile times for such experiments. When a company and its leaders frame a reaction to a crisis carefully and deliberately in line with their purpose, they will come out on the other side stronger, with supportive and united stakeholders and having delivered more positive impact.

Adapted from content posted on hbr.org, August 6, 2020 (product #H05RP4).

About the Contributors

BORIS BABIC is an assistant professor of decision sciences at INSEAD.

ALLISON BAILEY is a managing director and senior partner at Boston Consulting Group and the global leader of BCG's People and Organization practice.

BEA BOCCALANDRO is the author of *Do Good at Work: How Simple Acts of Social Purpose Drive Success and Well-being*, which was selected by three-time *New York Times*–bestselling author and Wharton professor Adam Grant as one of his 30 book recommendations. Bea also founded and runs VeraWorks, a global firm that advises companies on their social purpose efforts, and teaches corporate social purpose at Georgetown University and the University of Nevada, Las Vegas.

DANIEL L. CHEN is a professor at the Institute for Advanced Study at the Toulouse School of Economics and lead investigator at the World Bank's Data and Evidence for Justice Reform program.

PRITHWIRAJ (RAJ) CHOUDHURY is the Lumry Family Associate Professor at Harvard Business School. He was an assistant professor at Wharton prior to joining Harvard. His research is focused on studying the future of work, especially the changing geography of work. In particular, he studies the productivity effects of geographic mobility of workers, causes of geographic immobility, and productivity effects of remote work practices such as "work from anywhere" and "all-remote work."

FRANK COOPER III is a senior managing director, the global chief marketing officer, and a member of the global Executive Committee of BlackRock, the world's largest asset management company. His career has spanned entertainment (as senior executive at two of the world's most iconic music labels, Motown and Def Jam), technology (as chief marketing and creative officer at BuzzFeed), and consumer goods (as chief marketing officer of global consumer engagement for PepsiCo's global beverage group).

ERIN DOWELL is an equity and inclusion practitioner, investigator, and consultant. Erin advances organizational cultures of diversity, equity, and inclusion by developing policy, outreach, and education initiatives. She can be reached at hello@erindowell.com.

THEODOROS EVGENIOU is a professor of decision sciences and technology management at INSEAD.

ANNE-LAURE FAYARD is an associate professor of innovation, design, and organization studies at NYU's Tandon School of Engineering.

JOSEPH FULLER is a professor of management practice and a cochair of the Project on Managing the Future of Work at Harvard Business School. He is also the faculty cochair of HBS's executive education program on leading an agile workforce transformation.

RANJAY GULATI is the Paul R. Lawrence MBA Class of 1942 Professor of Business Administration at Harvard Business School.

MARLETTE JACKSON is a scholar, practitioner, and consultant of equity and social justice. Dedicated to removing barriers and providing equitable opportunity through systemic change, Marlette partners with organizations throughout the talent life cycle to promote a culture of inclusion and belonging. She is also cohost of *The FLI Collective*, a lifestyle podcast for women of color and former first-generation and/or low-income college students.

BRIAN KROPP is chief of research for the Gartner HR practice, which delivers insights and solutions that address new and emerging executive challenges and enable HR leaders to take decisive actions. Brian's expertise spans all aspects of HR, including talent acquisition and management, employee experience, change management, and leadership.

MANJARI RAMAN is a program director and senior researcher for Harvard Business School's Project on U.S. Competitiveness and the Project on Managing the Future of Work.

DEBORAH GRAYSON RIEGEL is a professional speaker, as well as a communication and presentation skills coach. She has taught for Wharton Business School, Columbia Business School, and Duke Corporate Education. She is the author of *Overcoming Overthinking: 36 Ways to Tame Anxiety for Work, School, and Life.*

GEORGE SERAFEIM is the Charles M. Williams Professor of Business Administration at Harvard Business School, a cofounder of KKS Advisors, and the chairman of Greece's

National Corporate Governance Council. He is an internationally recognized authority on ESG investing. Follow him on Twitter @georgeserafeim.

MICHAEL SLEPIAN is the Sanford C. Bernstein & Co. Associate Professor of Leadership and Ethics at Columbia Business School. Follow him on Twitter @michaelslepian.

NITHYA VADUGANATHAN is a managing director and partner at the Boston Consulting Group and a BCG Fellow on the Future of Work.

Index